Pra
Trans Anth~~ology~~ ~~Project~~

"What a gift to hear directly from transgender youth themselves about their gender journeys, as well as from parents navigating their own paths of self-discovery. The incredibly rich and diverse voices included in *Trans Anthology Project* offer comfort, compassion, and understanding, helping us become better parents to trans young people."

—Mandy Giles, Founder, Parents of Trans Youth

"*Trans Anthology Project* will open minds and touch hearts. Written by real people living with a broad spectrum of gender experiences beyond the binary, TAP educates the reader on the expansive nature of the transgender experience. Written with both strength and vulnerability, this Anthology encourages and challenges us all to consider the importance of progressive policies that will allow people to live their lives and families to support their children."

—Liz Schnelzer, LCSW, CCI, PFLAG Facilitator

"*Trans Anthology Project* does a remarkable job capturing the essence of what is gender-affirming care. By exploring key points that are often misunderstood by the general public, it provides an invaluable resource for anyone seeking to understand this critical aspect of healthcare better. The inclusion of personal stories from real patients and families helps to connect the reader on an emotional level, making the subject matter more relatable and impactful.

The author excels in explaining difficult, abstract subjects, using available evidence to demonstrate that gender diversity is not a new phenomenon but a natural part of human existence. This historical context is crucial in debunking myths and misconceptions surrounding gender diversity.

I plan to make this book required reading for any learners that rotate through our gender clinic. It serves as an excellent educational tool that

I believe will foster empathy and understanding in future healthcare providers. My hope is that the author's message reaches as many health-care clinicians as possible, at every level of the healthcare system, as well as families trying to figure out how best to support their loved ones going through similar experiences.

This anthology is not just a book; it is a beacon of knowledge and understanding, shedding light on the often misunderstood realm of gender-affirming care. Its impact on readers—both professional and personal—cannot be overstated."

—Jorge A. Ramallo, MD, Medical Director,
Inova Pride Clinic, Falls Church, VA

"*Trans Anthology Project* is a valuable resource, offering foundational information alongside heartfelt stories from parents, trans individuals, and providers. This collection, enriched with poetry and personal excerpts, serves as a vital source of insight and support for all who engage with it."

—Rebecca Minor, LICSW and Gender Specialist

"*Trans Anthology Project* is every bit as terrific, transparent, and trans-formative as I hoped it would be. Kirby's introduction is both disarming and enthralling. It reads as she speaks which gives power to possibility. As an educator and mental health professional, I find that the world speaks FOR children and teens rather than reminding them of the power and value of their own voices. TAP does what most educational books fail to do; trust the voices of the youth themselves to tell their own story. In doing so their voices show the complexity and simultaneous simplicity of gender, the full range of emotions, and the depth of their experiences. It is relatable and revolutionary, taking known experiences and showing them through unknown individuals who add depth and their own discovery which comes alive on the pages. Hearing the parents' initial uncertainties and compulsion towards protection followed by ultimate acceptance with simultaneous fear and willingness to push artificial boundaries to save their children is a journey *all* parents can relate to."

Though I suspect the people who will read this book are those who already know and love a trans person, those who are questioning their own gender identity, the parent of someone questioning such, or those educators and clinicians who already work with and teach trans youth; it is our politicians and adversarial groups who shout the loudest pseudoscience and say the least truth who really need to read such. How anyone can read the stories on these pages and fail to see the sheer beauty, courage, passion, intellect, and sincerity shared by the trans youth and their families while still questioning their value, validity, and indisputable authenticity is beyond me. To discount their voices and their stories is simply to *pretend* they don't exist. These voices are part of the beauty in our world and their lives need to be lived so their stories can continue being told."

—Amy Cannava, Ed.S., NCSP, Rainstorms to Rainbows

Trans Anthology Project

Reflections of Self-Discovery and Acceptance

Chrissy Boylan and
Heather H. Kirby, LCSW

PSYCHOLOGY / Gender
SELF-HELP / Gender & Sexuality

Authors: Chrissy Boylan and Heather H. Kirby, LCSW
Editor: Donna Mazzitelli, WritingWithDonna.com
Designer: Victoria Wolf, Wolf Design and Marketing
Publishing Consultant: Amy Colette, Unleash Your Inner Author, LLC

Website: https://www.transanthologyproject.com

Trans Anthology Project, Chrissy Boylan and Heather H. Kirby, LCSW. First edition.

Publisher: Trans Anthology Project

ISBN: 979-8-218-48950-2

*To all trans youth and families courageously
navigating a gender journey.*

And to those individuals who made this book possible by
contributing their stories, poems, and online reflections.

Contents

Introduction

THE TRANS ANTHOLOGY PROJECT was founded on the principle that while education can change minds, personal stories can change hearts. Stories have the power to touch people in the moment and leave a lasting impression. Through stories, we can step into the world of another and get a glimpse of what their life might be like. Stories can be truly transformative.

Now more than ever, the personal stories of transgender people need to be heard. In the last decade, gender diversity has entered our culture and our conversations in new and provocative ways. The issue has become politicized and polarized, and too often, we've lost sight of the individuals involved. According to a June 2022 Williams Institute Study, 1.6 million people in the US identify as transgender, 300,000 of which are between the ages of thirteen and seventeen.[1]

Yet those who came of age before the millennium likely grew up not knowing a single person who identified as transgender, non-binary, or gender queer, and may have only just become familiar with those terms in the last decade. Meanwhile, the younger generations have embraced and been exposed to these updated terms and concepts of gender from a young age and handle them with impressive dexterity. In general, today's youth accept gender diversity as a fact and interact with one another with little concern for gender or changes in gender identity or expression.

For the parents of trans and non-binary youth, teens, and young adults, this generational lack of exposure and knowledge can lead to misunderstanding, frustration, and fear. All across our country, there is a significant political and social discourse regarding the rights of trans people, and trans youth in particular. This discourse has become heated

---

1   https://williamsinstitute.law.ucla.edu/publications/trans-adults-united-states/

and, in some places, hateful. Many of those who are speaking loudly in the discourse have little to no personal experience of gender diversity.

The following provides some context for the "state" of our country based on available data from 2023.

By the Numbers

- **300,000:** the number of thirteen- to seventeen-year-olds who identify as trans or non-binary.

- **35%:** the percentage of thirteen- to seventeen-year-old trans and non-binary young people who live in states that have passed bans on gender-affirming care.

- **510:** the number of anti-LGBTQ+ bills introduced in state legislatures across the country in 2023, three times as many as in 2022.

- **84:** the number of anti-LGBTQ+ bills signed into law across twenty-three states in 2023 alone.

- **46%:** the percentage of thirteen- to seventeen-year-old trans and non-binary young people who considered suicide during 2023.

Data from Movement Advancement Project (MAP), ACLU, and The Trevor Project.

Regardless of your current beliefs, skepticism, religious objections, or personal encounters, gender diversity is now something you are likely hearing about and forming opinions about. We offer *Trans Anthology Project* to help provide a more personal perspective from which to form and inform your opinions.

You will find a diverse collection of stories, from both trans people and parents of trans people, depicting the many facets of gender exploration and discovery. With over thirty poems and essays written and submitted from people across the country, and 150 more voices represented through survey responses included throughout, we hope to convey the multitude of ways that teens and parents navigate the path to authenticity. More information on the contributors and additional survey responses can be found in the back of the book.

The poems and stories of personal experience are the heart of *Trans Anthology Project*. Educational content is provided at the beginning of each section to help place the personal accounts in a broader context and support readers in better understanding and appreciating each contributor's perspective. You will additionally find, "Thoughts from a Therapist," along the way offering Heather H. Kirby's firsthand clinical experiences from working with over one hundred trans youth and families during the last decade, as well as "Teen Talk" and "Parent Perspective," both of which are based on direct responses from our anonymous online surveys. Please note that in all cases the names have been changed to protect her clients' identities.

Trans Anthology Project is not meant to be an exhaustive educational guidebook. There are other resources, available online and offline, that provide more in-depth education on the science, history, and medical aspects of gender and transition. After interacting with the stories and content here, we encourage you to dive deeper into the topics that interest you.

This collection is presented in a natural order, offering a glimpse into the world of trans youth and their parents. While each section can stand alone and be read in any order, it can also be helpful to read the sections in the order presented. As you read, allow yourself to be touched and transformed by the stories of those who live with the experience of gender diversity.

It is our hope that within these pages, those who are on a gender journey (teens, young adults, and parents) will find validation and affirmation. In the stories that follow, we hope you discover the myriad of ways people explore, identify, disclose, and express their gender identity. There is no right way or wrong way to go about it, and no timeline, pace, or process works for everyone.

We acknowledge that no book of any length can fully capture the array of experiences held by gender-diverse people. If you do not find yourself in the pages of this book, or if the stories here do not seem to reflect your experience, please know this is due to the limitations of the book's length and not to anything you are doing wrong. You are on your own journey, at your own pace, and if you remain open, it will lead you to exactly where you are supposed to be.

If you are a trans teen: We hope you find in this book permission and encouragement to explore your gender identity. As you do, give yourself time and try not to rush the process or feel pressured to conform to others' ideas. When you are ready, and when it feels safe, claim your truth, knowing you are part of a vibrant community of resilient, courageous, intelligent, and creative people. Our intention is for the stories in the *Trans Anthology Project* to assure you that there is no *one* way to discover and proclaim your authentic self. There is no timetable and no criteria to meet.

We also hope that as you read the stories written by parents, you can appreciate that your parents are human and have their own reactions and feelings about what is happening. Gender diversity, as a concept, is newer to them, and they may naturally feel skeptical, as any of us tend to do when we learn new concepts. The sadness, angst, or grief they may be feeling is not about *you*.

It is their own way of processing what they are learning. They are concerned for your safety and well-being. The unknown is scary, and they may not be comfortable realizing you know more about gender diversity than they do. Be patient with them. Be direct with them about what you need. Take the time to let them hear what you have been learning about yourself. Trust that they care about and love you. And know that things will get better.

If you are a parent of a trans youth: We hope you will find comfort in the stories of other parents who have and are still traveling this bumpy road. We also hope you will find permission to feel all the emotions that might stir within you. There is no reason to feel guilty about any of your emotions. They merely indicate that you are human and have your own process as your child goes through theirs. Rarely will you and your child be in total sync as to what is happening and when. Be patient with yourself, and also with your child. This is not easy for them. This is not something they chose, and they are most likely in a lot of distress. Some kids appear depressed and others anxious or angry. They are trying to claim themselves in a world that seems to want to erase them. Take the time to learn what you need to know in order to feel comfortable moving forward, but realize that for your child, time is ticking. They are developing, and they know it. Their sense of urgency is real and needs to be considered.

If you are a family member, friend, ally, coach, therapist, faith leader, neighbor, teammate, colleague, or anyone who seeks deeper understanding: We hope this book will allow you to learn and better understand the challenges faced by trans youth and their families. We also hope it inspires empathy for the families who are navigating these murky waters. If you have not previously been an ally to the LGBTQ+ community, we unapologetically acknowledge our desire for this book to convert you to one. Our intention is that the *Trans Anthology Project* offers insights and cultivates compassion that might help all of us make the world a safer and more supportive place for trans youth. They are the most resilient, creative, courageous, and genuine people you will ever have the pleasure of knowing. One day, with deep gratitude, the world will look back and realize how much they have contributed to our society. Until then, they need people like you, in various areas of their lives, to accept, protect, and support them.

Terms and
Definitions

Just Embrace

Words are free
to hate or love.
To pull out roots
and chop above.
Or
to nurture and feed.
To grow that seed,
using love the world so desperately needs.
For the past is easy to fit in a mold,
but the future is vast and harder to hold.
To learn is to let that power unfold.
Knowledge.
Understanding.

Excerpt taken from *Just Embrace* by Rula Sinara

IN ORDER TO FULLY APPRECIATE the stories and information shared within the following pages, it is important to define a few terms up front. At the same time, please understand that the science, language, and culture surrounding gender is so fast-moving that updated terms and definitions evolve almost daily. As science continues to make strides in understanding gender diversity and new information becomes available, society takes note, replacing outdated terms with new terminology. In the meantime, the definitions and facts presented here are current to the best of our knowledge as of the publication date of this book.

Biological Sex, Gender, and Sexual Orientation

The single most important distinction to make first is between biological sex and gender, followed closely by the distinction between *either* biological sex or gender and sexual orientation.

Biological sex

Biological sex refers to the biological attributes, such as chromosomes, DNA, internal sexual organs, external genitalia, and hormonal make-up—i.e., tangible "things" that can be seen, measured, or put under a microscope. Biological sex is not so much determined as assigned, specifically at birth based on external genitalia. This assigned sex, either male or female, is then indicated by a sex marker on our birth certificate that follows us for the rest of our lives.

> **Assigned female at birth (AFAB):** a person who was observed to have external female genitalia and therefore designated as female at birth.

Assigned male at birth (AMAB): a person who was observed to have male genitalia and therefore designated as male at birth.

Gender

Unlike biological sex, gender is not something we can put under a microscope or "see." It is a complex phenomenon based on social, cultural, and personal factors that culminates in a sense of self as either man, woman, both, or neither. The concept of gender involves the interplay of three distinct components:

Gender role: the expected role of men versus women in any given society. This is purely a social construct as defined by one's culture. Gender roles vary greatly between different cultures and societies.

Gender identity: a deep, internal sense of self that stems from one's own thoughts, feelings, and preferences, that creates a view of who we are and how we relate to the world around us. Recent scientific studies suggest that gender identity is based on a complex neurochemical phenomenon that takes place in the brain. In a March 2018 TED Talk entitled, "Neither He, Nor She, But Me," writer, speaker, and gender activist Hannah Fons stated regarding gender identity, "This is what your soul feels like."[2]

Gender expression: the culmination of how we choose to present ourselves to the outside world. It includes what people see in our external expression, such as clothing choices, hair length and style, the accessories we wear, the hobbies we enjoy, and even the company we keep. It is important to realize that one's

2   https://www.ted.com/talks/hannah_fons_neither_he_nor_she_but_me/details

gender expression may or may not indicate their gender *identity*. There are a host of reasons why a person's identity and expression might be inconsistent, such as the need for physical safety or to safeguard one's mental health.

Sexual orientation

Refers *solely* to one's romantic or sexual attraction to another person. This can include heterosexual (straight), bisexual (bi), homosexual (gay or lesbian). There are some other, lesser-known orientations, such as pansexual (attracted to a wide range of identities) and asexual (having no sexual or romantic attraction) or demi-sexual (attracted sexually only after a close relationship has been established). Sexual orientation is completely separate from gender identity.

Cisgender, Transgender, Non-Binary, and Queer

The ways in which one can experience gender are infinite. So are the terms one can use to describe those experiences. At the highest level, we find it helpful to categorize the universe of gender identities into three fundamental types: cisgender, transgender, and queer.

Cisgender

When you have a gender identity that matches the sex you were assigned at birth, you are essentially *cisgender*. Many cisgender people are comfortable expressing their gender in ways that are expected and accepted by their culture. However, remember that gender expression and gender identity are two different things. A person might be cisgender and also express their gender in ways that are less common in their society.

Transgender

When you have a gender identity that does not align with the sex you were assigned at birth, you are transgender. This includes those who want to transition from one biological sex to the other (male to female or female to male), as well as those who live outside the constraints of the gender binary system altogether (non-binary).

Transgender male: a person assigned female at birth, who identifies as a male.

Transgender female: a person assigned male at birth, who identifies as a female.

Non-binary: a person assigned either male or female at birth but whose gender identity falls outside the construct of either male or female. Non-binary persons might further define their gender experience with more nuanced terms, such as *gender fluid, agender, bi-gender, gender non-conforming,* and more.

Queer
When you have a gender identity or sexual orientation that exists along a multidimensional spectrum such that the above labels and definitions are insufficient to describe your experience, you might fall under the flexible, catch-all umbrella term of queer.

Coming Out and Transitioning
Coming out and transitioning are extremely personal processes that take time, effort, and courage. And while many trans and non-binary teens tend to come out and socially transition at the same time, it's important to distinguish between the two. For instance, not all people who "come out" do so to everyone in their lives or in all settings, and not everyone who "comes out" will want to, are able to, or ready to transition.

Coming Out

Coming out is a reference to a person's brave disclosure of who they really are. The term indicates that a person has been going through an internal process of discovery and is now ready to share their truth. This may involve disclosure to one or more others and can be a lengthy process that, for some, never really ends. Because it takes courage to reveal a truth that might have been hidden, when one comes out to us, it is appropriate to thank them for trusting us.

Transitioning

At its essence, transitioning is the process of becoming more congruent inside and out. There are several aspects and levels of transition, primarily social, legal and medical. Each person's transition process and timeline are unique, and in service to becoming their most authentic and congruent self.

- The term "parent" is used to refer to anyone raising a gender-diverse youth.

- The term "trans" is used to refer to the larger umbrella of the gender-diverse community and is intended to be inclusive of all gender-diverse people, including transgender male, transgender female, non-binary, non-binary trans masc, non-binary trans femme, gender queer, gender fluid, and more.

What Is Gender Anyway?

Just Embrace

Control is a faulty goal.
It depletes and drains.
A muddy sinkhole.
It kills the spirit and tortures the soul
and
it takes its toll,
in life
or across the river Styx.
There is no magic or potion to mix
to fully heal the damage done
to needs neglected or children shunned.
Shun instead the poisonous hate.
The ignorance and judgment
It's not too late
Before it's too late

Just embrace

Excerpt taken from *Just Embrace* by Rula Sinara

GENDER AND ONE'S BIOLOGICAL SEX are separate and unique concepts.

While biological sex refers to biological and anatomical body parts, gender is a core component of our inner sense of self. Though we are born with an ineffable sense of our self, including gender identity, our gender expression is greatly influenced by the culture in which we live, our families of origin, and our lived experiences.

For example, in our modern Western culture, gender bias usually begins even before we are born. Soon-to-be parents hold "gender reveal parties" to celebrate the news that they are having a girl or a boy. From that point on, the colors of the nursery, the decorations, baby clothes, and toys all tend to have a gender tilt. For boys, there is the color blue, clothes that are generally pants and shirts, and toys that center around vehicles and tools. For girls, there is the color pink, frilly dresses, and toys that center around dolls and housekeeping. If we think about the implicit messages received by newborns from the day they arrive, we can easily see how cultural norms around gender become internalized.

Even the most liberal parents, the staunchest feminists, and the most progressive dads fall prey to these cultural trends. This idea of gender is so ingrained in our society that we might miss the reality that the assignment of colors, toys, and clothing styles attributed to boys or girls is wholly arbitrary.

Let's look at how gender identity is shaped, influenced, and discovered.

Gender Identity in Early Life

As a newborn, we don't really know or care what sex we were assigned at birth. We are swaddled, bathed, fed, and loved the same whether assigned boy or girl. Only as we age do we begin learning the differences between girls and boys and the "rules" for being either one, such as what one should wear, which hairstyles are appropriate, how one should act, and which toys and activities one should enjoy.

Some gender-diverse kids will announce their emerging sense of gender diversity at a very young age. They are clear and adamant about the fact that they are "really a girl" or "really a boy" regardless of their assigned sex. Only a few decades ago, these children would have been sent to therapy while their parents worked hard at home to get them to conform to social expectations. In many areas of our country, this is still the case.

Other gender-diverse kids may feel "different" but lack the words or concepts to understand or communicate their budding sense of gender diversity. And other gender-diverse kids won't discover their gender identity until puberty or beyond.

Preschool

By age four or five, some kids show a rejection of gender norms. Girls who don't conform to feminine expectations or who seem to enjoy more "boyish" things might be called a "tomboy" at this age. Likewise, boys who do not play rough and tumble, or who do not seem to conform to the male gender expectations might be called "sensitive" or "quiet."

However, not all kids who defy gender norms are gender diverse. Nor are those who adhere to gender norms necessarily cisgender. For example, some gender-diverse kids will feel different but won't know how or won't want to express it. In fact, some try to actively hide or ignore it. These kids may try hard to fit in, sometimes even exaggerating their gender compliance in an effort to embrace expectations. For this reason, many parents upon learning that their kid is gender diverse, will report, "We had no clue; there were no signs; they seemed so happy as a child." And for a while, they probably were happy because following gender norms brought on the approval of parents and teachers and feeling included among their peers. Eventually, however, most gender-diverse kids will reach a point in their development where they can no longer avoid the truth of their gender diversity.

Elementary School Years

By primary school, the differences between genders are accentuated and the rules become more explicit and rigid. Teachers will say phrases such as, "Boys line up over here, and girls over there," "Young ladies don't sit like that," or "Boys don't wear dresses or makeup." Children who uphold these expectations are often rewarded with smiles, proud parents, and the acceptance of their peers. Those who don't conform are instead met with skeptical looks, frustrated parents, and possible alienation from their peers. Kids of all gender identities learn rather early that there are costs to being different and rewards for conforming to expectations.

Middle School Years

In middle school, the lines grow even sharper. Girls gather in groups to talk about how "gross" boys are. Boys gather to plan pranks on girls. The expectations are so clear that many gender-diverse kids assume there is something wrong with them and may try to hide their true gender identity lest they risk social embarrassment or stigma. These kids "go along to get along" and often try to play by the rules to reap the social rewards. Until they enter puberty.

Puberty and Gender Dysphoria

At puberty, the body begins to change and develop secondary sex characteristics. This is an uncomfortable time for most teens and tweens, regardless of gender identity. For example, many girls become embarrassed by their budding breasts or wish they didn't have monthly cramps and bleeding. Many boys are often confused and embarrassed by "wet dreams" or spontaneous erections.

For some kids, puberty is what triggers the realization that they might be gender diverse.

For other kids who already suspected, knew, or fully owned their gender diversity, puberty can accentuate the tension between their gender identity and biological sex that much more. As their body begins to change, both groups tend to feel a disconnect between the direction their body is moving and their internal sense of self. This can be so confusing and upsetting that many kids are reluctant to share their awareness. Many report that they just hoped it would "go away."

As puberty progresses and physical changes grow, so do the realizations that their bodies will become more like a biological man or a woman, whether they want it to or not. The discomfort and distress caused by this disconnect can become profoundly intense and cause mental distress. For some, having a body that is maturing into an identity that doesn't match their inner sense of self can feel like a runaway train. The prospect of having to live the rest of their life "stuck" in a body that doesn't match their gender identity can feel overwhelming. Often, this distress leads to depression, anxiety, school avoidance, eating disorders, drug use, or self-harm. For example, gender-diverse kids report the highest level of suicidal ideation, with over 40 percent of gender-diverse kids saying they have considered or attempted suicide.

This intense distress is known as gender dysphoria, a complicated term that means something different to each person and can be felt both physically and socially.

Thoughts from a Therapist ...

One client, John, really summed up what I had heard from countless kids. He said, "When I was younger, I just figured I didn't fit in well with the other girls. But I was accepted as a tomboy and so it didn't really bother me too much. But when I started getting breasts and my period, it felt totally wrong. That's when I felt like there was something really wrong with me. I got pretty depressed and avoided a lot of social activities. I just felt really wrong in my body. When I learned about transgender, it pretty quickly clicked for me that that is what I had been feeling all along."

Physical Dysphoria

Physical dysphoria is a bodily experience. It is a disturbing awareness that one's body is fundamentally different from one's sense of self. The type, level, and degree of physical dysphoria varies among individuals. For some, it is mild, and for others, it can be truly debilitating. For some, the dysphoria comes and goes, and for others, their physical dysphoria is ever-present. For some, the degree of discomfort may vary depending on the situation and context (at home, among friends, in public, etc.), and for others, it is everywhere, all the time.

Though every gender-diverse person's experience is different, the three main sources of physical dysphoria tend to be:

Genitalia and secondary sex characteristics

One's genitalia is often reported as the primary source of physical dysphoria. However, secondary sex characteristics, such as breast development or facial hair, can create intensifying dysphoria as one goes through puberty. For example, the presence of developing breast tissue may be a source of distress for those assigned female who identify as male, while facial hair is often a source of concern for those assigned male who identify as female.

Height

Teens assigned male at birth whose growth spurt might have rendered them taller than the average female might be extremely self-conscious about their height. On the other hand, kids assigned female at birth may become upset at the realization that they are unlikely to achieve the height of an average male.

Voice

Once the voice deepens through the process of puberty, it will never revert to a higher register. For some kids assigned male at birth, this is a significant source of distress. No matter how much they transition physically, they feel like their voice betrays them and indicates to others that they were assigned male at birth. Similarly, at a certain age, trans males feel significant distress by the higher register of their voice that did *not* change during puberty. Voice dysphoria leads some kids to be extremely reluctant to speak up, or to even speak at all. Some trans teens will choose to withhold all speech in order to avoid hearing their own voice.

GENDER-DIVERSE YOUNG PEOPLE will go to great lengths to manage and deal with this physical distress that centers around various areas of their physical body. Many wear baggy clothes to obscure their developing body. Some will avoid looking in mirrors, and when their physical distress becomes extremely intense, it can prevent kids from wanting to shower, go to school, or leave their bedroom.

Social Dysphoria

Social dysphoria refers to the distress associated with having to live up to the social expectations and norms of one's perceived gender. For some transgender individuals, these social expectations are the most disturbing aspect of gender dysphoria. Some kids will describe that they can "live with the body" they have but cannot tolerate the gender expectations placed on them. It is more distressing for some to be referred to in gendered ways (girl, boy, he, she, young man, ma'am, etc.) than it is to deal with their body's development.

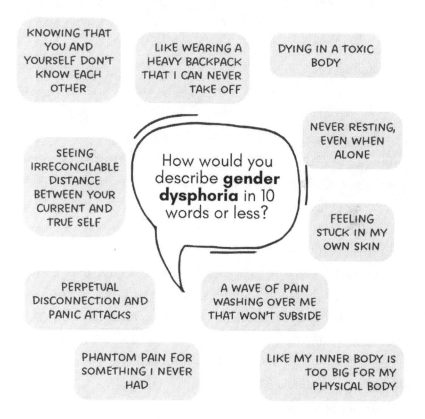

Thoughts from a Therapist ...

In a recent group meeting of gender-diverse tweens, three of the five reported that they "hate gym class," not because they do not enjoy sports or recreation, but because their gym teacher routinely divides the group between boys and girls. Since they identify as non-binary, they tend to sit out. They reported feeling worried that this might draw the attention of bullies. They also reported that while they otherwise liked their gym teacher who was "nice," they were very hurt that there was no attempt to change the divide so they could participate.

Exploring One's Gender Identity

For those gender-diverse kids not yet aware, it is often the experience of gender dysphoria, physical or social, that spurs them to question and explore their gender identity.

The Internet is a true gift to these kids. Without ever having to reveal themselves to anyone, they can research and learn, discovering other trans and gender-diverse individuals and realizing they are not alone. They can also join online communities where they feel accepted and gain the strength and support they need to eventually come out when they are ready and feel safe to do so.

Most of this Internet research and soul-searching goes on behind closed doors and in secret. Most kids do not want to share their suspicion of being trans before they have done private exploration on their own.

At this point in the journey, kids typically fall into one of two camps. In one camp are those who decide to tell someone that they suspect they are transgender. They know full well that this act of disclosure will lead to a difficult path of unknowns. These youth courageously step out and announce their truth and live with integrity to who they really are. In the other camp are those kids who decide that the risks are too great, and they will keep their secret while trying even harder to live as their assigned sex. They, too, know full well that theirs will not be an easy path. These kids know that they will continue to feel uncomfortable and that they are suppressing a huge piece of themselves. But, for them, the alternative may feel impossible.

The kids in BOTH camps are strong and courageous. The difference lies not in the teen's character, resolve, or degree of certainty regarding their gender identity but more likely their sense of relative safety.

teen talk

What would you say to your younger self?

- You don't have to figure stuff out right away.

- Be yourself.

- Know you are loved and will always be loved no matter what.

- Don't force yourself into a box that society has created. They don't know the true you.

- Things get better. You are stronger, braver, and smarter than you think you are. You will get through the hard times.

- Don't worry kid, we will not be lost forever, the day will come soon when we find our way back home.

- There is no one universal experience or narrative you have to follow in order to be trans. Everyone's journey and experience with their gender is different.

- Love yourself and get off the internet.

- Don't frown upon the kids that are not like you. Gay, lesbian, and queer are not dirty words. Keep an open mind and learn more about the LGBTQ+ community; you may become a part of it when you get older. ;)

- Come out as soon as you know it is safe for you. Don't hide it.

Non-Binary Identities

Non-binary is a general term that captures the multitude of gender experiences that lie outside the binary of male and female. There are numerous terms used to describe the unique and nuanced experiences of gender. Some people use *gender fluid* or *gender flux* to describe their gender as vacillating between the binary of male and female. For others, gender is experienced as neither male nor female, often labeled *agender* or *genderless*. One might identify partly (but not fully) with a binary gender and use the label *demiboy* or *demigirl*. Some might identify as non-binary and acknowledge a preference for a certain gender presentation by using the terms *transmasc* or *transfemme*. Still, others might prefer the broader and more inclusive label of *gender queer*. New terms and labels will continue to emerge to best capture the many nuanced experiences of gender outside of a binary construct.

> **What any one person means when they use a term to describe their gender identity might differ from another person using the same term. The only way to know what a person really means is to ask them what that term means *for them*.**

As exposure and education on gender diversity continues to grow, more people are finding a non-binary description that fits their identity. In fact, within the trans community, one-third identify as non-binary. However, while non-binary is often considered a subcategory under the broader umbrella of transgender, not all non-binary people identify as trans.

There is no wrong or right way to be non-binary; it is a deeply personal and nuanced experience of one's gender identity, and all expressions should be respected and acknowledged as valid without judgment or expectations.

Non-binary people often face significant hardships from living outside antiquated societal norms and expectations. Because they do not identify as either male or female, many non-binary persons use neutral pronouns (such as "they/them") that feel unfamiliar, and even uncomfortable, for some. Because most of our society defaults to the binary way of thinking, non-binary people are frequently misgendered, even by friends and family. This invalidation can cause psychological distress and emotional pain. However, the challenges faced by non-binary persons go beyond misgendering.

Non-binary people navigate daily obstacles related to our binary-based culture, including bathroom usage, dress codes, educational settings, sports participation, children's toys, employment, titles and salutations, and even the use of identification documents. Even gender-affirming medical treatments can be challenging for non-binary individuals due to limited options and biased medical systems.

Credit is owed to Dr. Kori Saunders, PsyD, MA, who contributed greatly to this segment by sharing their expertise on non-binary identities.

Thoughts from a Therapist ...

I remember working with a group of teens, and one of the non-binary kids was trying to explain why they felt it was even harder to be non-binary than to be trans male or trans female. They pointed out that most people assume that you are either male or female. They noted that a trans person can make changes that steer others in the right direction so that they are recognized as male or female. Then they said, "Every day, I have to decide which assumption I will hate the least." It took me a minute to decipher this statement. They knew that an assumption would be made about them, and they didn't like either the assumption of male or female. Depending on how they felt that day, one of those assumptions would be a bit worse than the other. That statement has stuck with me as I work with non-binary teens. Our society continues to see a binary world of men and women, and for non-binary people, this is a daily struggle.

Enough Already

I'M SIX YEARS OLD. My grandfather gives my two younger sisters and me toy trucks for Christmas. It's the dawn of the 1970s, but I do not see this as an enlightened, progressive gesture. I experience it as evidence of disappointment, an attempt to mold us into the boys we clearly are not. I try my best to play with the trucks, but dolls and toy kitchens feel more right to me.

I'm nine years old. My sisters and I have chickenpox and are home from school, swaddled under blankets, tattooed with Calamine lotion, sipping ginger ale. My paternal grandmother sits with us while my mother runs an errand. She's in one of her moods, despairing of her lot in life and miserable with the world for all the ways it has failed her. Today, it is we who have failed her, as she laments how unfortunate it is that the three of us were born female. "I wish just one of you could have been a boy," she wails, judging us unfit to adequately help with the family business. I feel tears well up. As the oldest, I am the first disappointment. I am so sorry, I mouth silently.

Weeks pass, and the shame becomes overwhelming. I cry in bed at night, and my mother comes to see what's wrong. I confess that I've discovered the family secret of disappointment in me, and I apologize for my inadequacy. I don't know if this revelation makes her angry or sad. She assures me I am loved just as I am, but I hear none of it.

I will spend decades fighting the shame and proving myself.
I will spend decades believing that I am not enough.

I'm eleven years old. I sit in my empty sixth-grade classroom while the rest of the class is outside. Two weeks earlier, the principal announced plans for an ad hoc soccer game against a nearby school. The boys will play soccer; the girls will be cheerleaders.

I am outraged at this injustice. Boys get to play an exciting, high-stakes game; girls are relegated to the sidelines, our only job is to cheer on the boys as they do battle. I chafe at the traditional gender roles and refuse to be a cheerleader. There is no girl power yet. Title IX is slowly making its way across the country but hasn't stopped in my town. So, while my classmates assemble on the field, the boys practicing passes, the girls perfecting saucy choreographed moves, I sit in the empty classroom, alone.

I'm sixteen years old. I work in the public library, and every day in another section of the shelves, a new door opens for me. I read *The Second Sex* and *The Feminine Mystique*. I use my paycheck to buy a subscription to *Ms. Magazine*. There is no going back.

I'm eighteen. I go to college in another part of the country, and I'm mystified by many of the women I meet. They put on a full face of makeup to go check the dorm mailbox. They dress in skirts and heels and add-a-bead necklaces for sorority rush. Their hair is always perfectly coiffed. They openly talk about getting their Mrs. degree. They don't swear like I do. I'm in T-shirts and jeans and a spiky punk haircut, and I call myself the dirtiest of all words, a feminist. For four years, I never feel like I fit in.

I'm twenty years old. I'm taking Women's Studies 101 this semester, and I'm writing a paper on children and gender roles.

I find a book in the college library on raising children free from traditional stereotypes. It's not academic; it's parenting advice, and I devour it. It's a revelation. This is what I'm going to do, I pledge. I'll give my daughter a truck and my son a doll, and they'll always know they are enough.

I'm forty-three. The fertility treatment was a bust, and I'm hunched over a thick stack of papers, an application from an international adoption agency. The agency allows you to specify a gender preference, and I write "no preference," knowing that this almost guarantees I'll be matched with a boy. Girls are in much more demand in international adoption, and the wait is long. I'm finished with waiting. I want to be a mom. My "no preference" is a preference, though. I prefer not to relive the toxicity our culture rains down on girls. I prefer not to watch a daughter get diminished by every micro-aggression and lesser expectations. Instead, I will raise one of the good guys. A sensitive, respectful man. I believe this is my calling.

Or is my "no preference" choice of a son a way to win the approval of my long-dead grandparents? I'm not ready to go there. I move on to the next question on the application form.

My son is two. We bring him to the United States, and he settles into his gender-neutral, rainforest-themed bedroom. I try to find little boy clothes that are not sports-themed, but it's hard. We buy him toy trucks and cars, but also a play kitchen and stuffed animals. I cuddle and kiss and hug him far longer than I see other mothers with sons do. He sneaks into our bed at night and wraps a little arm around my neck. I love saying that he's a "mama's boy."

My son is seven. All of his friends are girls. We try to get him into boys' soccer, but he's the tiniest child on the team and is terrified when boys twice his size charge him. We realize he doesn't pal around with the boys in his class. I congratulate myself. He's seeing girls as equal, not lesser. If I'm worried at all about not having male friends, I know this will all change soon enough, in later childhood when girls and boys naturally gravitate to their own genders for a while.

My son is nine. He wants nothing for Christmas but an American Girl doll. We visit the American Girl doll store, and he's embarrassed, the only boy in a sea of girls in the crowded store, but he's also devouring the dolls with his eyes. I make up a game. "Let's pretend we're shopping for Sophia's birthday," I say, using his best friend as our cover. "We can look at the dolls and say to each other, 'I wonder if she would like this?'" And we do. We spend more than an hour in the store, examining every display, scrutinizing every outfit, accessory, shoe. He's delighted, not self-conscious. On Christmas morning, he unwraps a blond American Girl doll. I've given my family a heads-up, and my sister's present to him is a number of tiny outfits.

My son is eleven. He won't agree to a haircut, asking instead if he can grow his hair long. As every restaurant server asks, "What would you like, miss?" I wonder if we've made the right decision. I don't notice how good this is making him feel.

My son is twelve. He sleeps all the time. His grades are slipping. We attribute all of this to the transition to middle school, which we understand can be rough. It doesn't get better. He hints that he has a secret but can't tell us what it is.

My son is thirteen. We're a few months into the school year, and the school counselor and I have been trying to address the bad grades, the sleeping during class, but nothing is working. Then the counselor calls me and says that he's learned that my son's friends are referring to him as "she" and "her." I don't know anything about pronouns yet. Later, I'll learn how to ask and give my own in virtually any setting. For now, though, as a truth begins to dawn on me, I push it down with denial and bargaining with God. I am adrift. I take my son to a psychologist and, in our family session, the psychologist asks if my son would like to discuss gender identity. He looks down at his shoes and is silent.

My son is thirteen. It's a few days before Christmas. He and I are alone in the house. He tells me it's time for him to tell me his secret. I am certain I know, but I wait for him to say it. In that millisecond before he speaks, I am flooded with love so electric it crackles. He is not going to be burdened by who he is, with not being enough.

"I think I'm really a girl," he says, searching my face wildly for my reaction. I pull her to me and kiss the top of her head. I tell her that I'm proud of her for telling me, that it took a lot of courage. I assure her that she is loved, and that there is nothing, there will never be anything, that will change that.

My daughter is fourteen. She wears only hoodies and sweat-pants, her year-round uniform since she was six. I'm perplexed—in an effort to demonstrate my unequivocal support and acceptance, I've bought her bras, panties, feminine pj's, and cute tops. They sit untouched in her dresser drawers. It's okay—we're homebound by a global pandemic. But then, one day, it all clicks, with makeup. She spends hours watching YouTube makeup tutorials. I grab my purse, excited to help her usher in her newfound gender expression, and we head, masked, to Walgreens, to Sephora, to Ulta. She tells me she needs concealer and highlighter, and I tell her I don't even know what those potions do. Her daily skincare routine involves nine products more than my bar of soap. She buys eyeshadow palettes and eyeliner. She dyes her hair a rainbow of colors before returning back to jet black. She is beautiful. She was always beautiful, but now, to my unease, after perfecting a look that media images have taught her is the most desirable, she believes it.

My daughter is fifteen. She wears crop tops that show off her hourglass figure and a full face of makeup and false eyelashes. She constantly asks me how she looks—is her foundation the right shade, is her tummy bloated, is her hair too dry, how's her eyeliner? She talks about the need for plastic surgery—to have her nose reshaped, her cheeks lifted, her lips made fuller. She hands me her phone to see the latest Instagram influencer and asks me to compare her appearance against a professionally styled and airbrushed image. She has absorbed every toxic message our culture serves up to teenage girls. I worry that she measures her worth only by her appearance. I say all the things you're supposed to say, about her intelligence, her resilience, her strength. I try to steer her to different role models. I worry she hears none of it. I worry she will spend her life thinking she is not enough.

—B

My Gender Exploration

EVERY PERSON'S STORY of gender exploration is unique, and a lack of diverse representation can make the experience even more alienating. For example, on social media, television, and in books, the stories I heard were of transgender individuals who always felt different from other people of their assigned gender or had long wondered about the gender constructs of society. I, on the other hand, fit perfectly into the female stereotype until around the age of eleven. I hated boys and loved pink, unicorns, skirts, and *Frozen*. Although I also liked minions and dinosaurs and wasn't as huge of a Disney fan as most other girls.

During my preteen era, I cut off over a foot of my hair to donate to a cancer wig program. Despite the strange looks I received in the women's restrooms about my short hair, I still identified as a girl. Around that same time, I also stopped liking dresses and other stereotypical feminine hobbies, and instead became more interested in playing rough sports with the boys at school. Even then, I still identified as a girl.

That summer, when I was almost twelve, my best friend confessed that she had a crush on me, which led me to question my sexuality. I went through a myriad of labels, such as lesbian and bisexual, as I realized I cared deeply about her in a way that I thought was romantic. By age twelve, I was dipping my toes in the waters of LGBTQ+ identities and eventually became aware that I was not a girl at all, contrary to my previous identification as a tomboy. I experimented with many gender identities, including non-binary and genderfluid, before settling on the general category of the masculine range of the non-binary spectrum.

A key part of this journey for me was gender dysphoria, which I started feeling when I was twelve or thirteen. This discomfort was particularly overwhelming regarding my chest and reproductive system. Ever since learning of the menstrual cycle when I was nine, the mere thought of getting a period horrified me, sometimes to the point of a complete shutdown. I never connected the dots, however, until I was almost thirteen. The gender dysphoria got so bad I had to take showers in a swimsuit with the lights turned off so I couldn't see my body. Fortunately, I started hormone blockers before I started menstruating, which significantly decreased the dysphoria I felt.

Today, in 2023, after being on testosterone for over a year, my physical dysphoria is almost nonexistent, but I still have many anxieties and social dysphoria about my body language and gender roles in teenage society. I'm a sophomore in high school and have been going to school stealth, or presenting as a cis male, since seventh grade. This has worked well for me so far, especially after I started HT, though I often feel on edge for fear of being found out.

Some of the most positively influential moments in my transition were learning about the vast LGBTQ+ community online and through other transgender peers, as well as receiving incredible support from my family and medical providers. I hope that in telling my story, other transgender individuals may also find guidance or connection. Because in this stressful world, as politicians actively campaign to take away our basic human rights, it is more important than ever to stand together as a community. Sharing my story and being available to aid those who are struggling is my way of supporting my trans siblings.

—Sixteen-Year-Old Trans Masc

(Gender) Message Received

AS A SIXTEEN-YEAR-OLD TRANS GUY reflecting on my childhood, I remember receiving various early messages about how boys and girls should behave and what was expected of them. These messages often came from my family, friends, media, and society as a whole. Here are some of the key messages I recall:

1. Toys and interests: From an early age, I noticed that certain toys and activities were deemed appropriate for boys and girls. Boys were encouraged to play with action figures, cars, and sports-related toys, while girls were expected to enjoy dolls, kitchen sets, and arts and crafts. These distinctions in toy choices reinforced the idea that boys should be active and competitive, while girls should be nurturing and creative.

2. Appearance and dress: Society often conveyed that boys and girls should adhere to specific dress codes. Boys were supposed to wear "masculine" clothing such as pants, shirts, and sneakers, while girls were expected to wear dresses, skirts, and more "feminine" attire. These early expectations regarding clothing reinforced traditional gender roles.

3. Emotions and expressiveness: I learned that boys were supposed to be tough and stoic, encouraged to suppress their emotions and not cry. On the other hand, girls were known to be more emotional and expressive, and it was acceptable for them to show vulnerability. These messages left me feeling pressured to hide my emotions.

4. Social roles: I noticed that adults often assigned specific roles and responsibilities based on gender. Boys were expected to take on more active roles, like helping with physical tasks or being the protector, while girls were often encouraged to focus on caregiving and domestic responsibilities. These early messages reinforced stereotypes about traditional gender roles within the family and society.

5. Communication styles: I observed differences in how boys and girls were encouraged to communicate. Boys were expected to be assertive and direct, while girls were often encouraged to be polite, accommodating, and nurturing in their interactions. These communication patterns influenced my understanding of how I should interact with others.

6. Career aspirations: Adults occasionally made remarks about potential future careers based on gender. Boys were sometimes told they should aspire to careers in fields like science, technology, engineering, and mathematics (STEM), while girls were often nudged toward professions that were considered more nurturing or service-oriented. These messages can limit career choices and perpetuate gender disparities.

7. Sports and physical activities: I noticed that boys were often pushed toward competitive sports and physical activities, while girls were sometimes encouraged to focus on less competitive forms of exercise. These expectations can create a divide in opportunities for physical activity and competition.

8. Peer influence: My peers also played a significant role in reinforcing gender expectations. I observed that conforming to these expectations was often seen as a way to fit in and avoid social ridicule. This peer pressure added to the challenges of navigating my gender identity.

However, I openly defied these messages and rules because they never resonated with who I truly was. I wasn't interested in the toys or activities that society deemed appropriate for girls. I wanted to climb trees, play with action figures, and explore my own interests. I didn't care for the stereotypes that suggested I should be timid or passive. Instead, I wanted to be assertive, confident, and true to myself.

I began to dress and present myself in a way that felt authentic to who I was. I didn't conform to traditional gender expectations but rather followed my heart. I found a supportive community of friends who accepted me for who I was, and I sought out mentors and role models who had also defied gender norms.

—Anonymous

Two Crescent Moons

(1)

He was named out of necessity. The atoms colliding in my new and volatile universe were too fast and too hot. Ray condensed from these overwhelming desires and was born my North Star.

Young and bright, I couldn't look away, let alone forget his shine.

I see Polaris gleam when he's in the mirror and total darkness when I've forsaken us both.

(2)

Ray is like my twin yet behaves like a younger brother. Maybe there was a time when we were one being, before the Big Bang. But then we were torn apart, thrust into different worlds, like two moons always orbiting out of phase with one another.

He's the version of myself that I see in fleeting moments in the mirror. Sometimes he's so close that I can feel what he feels. Sometimes he's so far away that no matter how long I look at my reflection, I only see me.

He's living his best life, and I'm stuck on this side, unable to join.

I'm jealous of him; so, so jealous that I turn angry, gritting my teeth as I wipe away my tears. He doesn't know what he did wrong; his face suggests panic.

For all I know, he might want to be me too.

We lie in the fetal position face-to-face, becoming two crescent moons.

Why would you ever want to be me? There's nothing left here for you, I cry.

But all he does is stare.

(3)
Ray comes to me in the bus window. He materializes the moment I realize that no one on this bus understands the feeling of being the only person who can comfort you through your own reflection.

He stares back at me. He's taking the same bus, too, just in his homologous, parallel world.

I tell him, with my "older sister" tone, *we're the only two people who can understand. No one would ever be able to come as close as you and I.* He nods and fades away as the bus drives off.

(4)

Summer afternoon. I've woken up late again.

My body feels terrible. Too restless to stay in bed but too tired to get up. I roll to my side and pretend Ray is there, forming our crescent moons. He's as tired as I am.

Would you come here and rot with me, together into one corpse lying in the forest, and wait for the fungi to take us?

Yes, he says. He smiles, and I smile too.

(5)

In my dreams, Ray has an undercut. In my waking hours, I touch where hair meets nape and wish my long hair would magically trim itself off.

I know it's inevitable that he'll come into my world more often and I won't be able to ignore it. He's as stubborn as me, after all.

Is there a way for you to grow without burying me? Is there a way for me to live without killing you?

I search for him through the rain-covered window. He sits in his favorite sunflower dress, eyes watery, ever so patiently waiting for me to answer.

(6)
Ray is the moon, the stars. He's my nourishment, my poison; my joy, my sadness.

But I'm still hoping for the day someone calls his name,

And I can turn around and say, "Yes, that's me."

—Ray JC Chang

Living In the Gray Zone

OUR WORLD IS SET UP in binaries: black/white, hot/cold, up/down, yes/no, left/right, male/female. My non-binary child is not.

They were born on a warm day in February, after a long day of laboring. Right at the time when we would normally be picking up their older brother from daycare, our new bundle of joy emerged into the world.

Ironically, we had decided to find out the sex of our second baby. We had wanted to be surprised with our first pregnancy but could barely handle not knowing by the end. We also wanted to know about our second baby so we could inform their older brother.

A baby shower was thrown for me, and almost everything was shades of pink. So much pink! We had a shorter list of names this time—only girl names. By the second day after giving birth, we had given the baby a name, confident it was fitting.

However, our assigned female at birth child emerged at around thirteen years old as NOT A GIRL. Their birth name was rejected, and several chosen names tried on. They were non-binary, gender fluid, neither male nor female but somewhere on the spectrum between. One day they wore eye makeup and wanted to be pretty. Other days they donned a suit jacket with tie and wanted to be handsome. A shorter haircut, a binder to minimize their chest, and they/them pronouns. Transitioning to their true self was termed "brave." "They are so courageous," one person said.

What they are is scared and trying to live their truth. They are both anxious and worried about how others perceive them. They have found some solace with others who identify as transgender, but along with their grayness on our culture's black/white spectrum comes sadness.

Will someone use my deadname?

Will someone misgender me?

What bathroom should I use in public?

More than gender fluid, they are a teenager with all the angst and fears that come with this phase. They are moody and experience relationship difficulties like everyone else. Some days are better than others. Going to the store to buy clothing, for example, can be triggering. We purchase boxer briefs, but sports bras are more difficult.

My child has the right to be comfortable in their own skin, and not be defined by a false binary or someone's legislative whims. Living in the gray zone isn't pink or blue or even purple. It is a beautiful shade of gray, and that's okay.

—Carol

The History
and Biology of
Gender Diversity

Just Embrace

Nature didn't get it wrong.
The air vibrates with bird song.
From countless species and colors of wings,
every bird ... every being ... has the right to sing.
To live and stretch and fly high.
There is no right or wrong or why.
Each song resonates with a different soul.
From birth to death, a different goal.
From seed and egg, a destiny.
Just let it be.
There is nothing more fundamental to life,
more precious or beautiful,
than diversity.
Don't blame nature.

It's society

With boxes and rules and expectations,
to quell the fear of variation
of darkness and the unknown.
But we've boldly been where no man has gone
before.
So, what more?
What's needed to understand
that when our children feared the dark
we took their hand.
We held them through the night.
We didn't question wrong or right.
Because we knew that at the heart of the matter,
it didn't matter.
Only love mattered.

We just embraced.

Excerpt taken from *Just Embrace* by Rula Sinara

THERE ARE ENTIRE BOOKS WRITTEN about the history of the binary and the enforcement of gender roles during the spread of Western civilization and colonialization. There are also books about the various ways that gender diversity is celebrated in other cultures as a positive and natural variation of the human experience as well as books about the biology of sex and gender. For our purposes, we want to provide an overview for your reference and understanding as you take in the personal stories. For more detailed information on any of the topics covered in this section, we encourage you to seek out additional resources.

Not a New Phenomena

Gender diversity has existed throughout history in a variety of cultures. So why does it seem new to us? Because gender diversity was largely erased during colonialization.

It's important to remember that gender is a social construct and that all social constructs are defined by the prevailing culture of the time. Gender is not, in other words, something rooted in objective reality or nature, and the idea that gender is binary, that one can only ever be male or female as determined by genitalia, turns out to be an invention of Western civilization. In fact, prior to the spread of Western civilization ideals, gender diversity was a biological truth that was celebrated across species, space, and time.

In humans specifically, gender diversity can be traced back to several ancient cultures, including Mesopotamia, Greece, and India. For thousands of years, gender-diverse people were allowed to flourish and were revered and celebrated. In India, for example, *hijras* have been recognized as a third gender since at least 400 CE. Historically based in Hinduism, hijras are held in high regard and thought to bring blessings of fertility, prosperity, and longevity. Among various Indigenous North American cultures, those who expressed and performed functions of both sexes were referred to as Two-Spirits. One such example is the lhamana of the Zuni Tribe in New Mexico. Like the hijras, lhamana people were celebrated and given explicit ceremonial roles to represent balance and stability within their culture. There are also the Bugis in Indonesia, Muxes in Mexico, Sekrata in Madagascar, the Hawaiian Māhū, and several more.

Things changed with the spread of Christian ideals of patriarchy and Western colonialism. From about the fifteenth century on, Western colonialists forced the idea of the gender binary, among other ideologies, onto the cultures they colonized as a tool of power and influence. Those in power set deliberately strict and rigid definitions of what it meant to be a "man" or "woman" as a way of framing these other cultures as unrefined and in need of Western ideas. Considering that by 1914, Europe had colonized up to 80 percent of the world, you can see how a social construct can take on a life of its own.

The gender binary, the idea that one can only either be man or woman, was further reinforced during the Enlightenment Era, when scholars and scientists of the time used the shroud of science to uphold societal norms. Gender was equated with biological sex, and biological sex became an "objective" and binary "fact" of anatomy.

By ostracizing those outside the gender binary, Western colonization essentially erased the roles of, and words to describe, trans and non-binary people. These groups became marginalized as the dominant culture adopted the notion of a gender binary. Over time, it became so established that it was accepted as truth, and many of us grew up not knowing the storied history of gender diversity through the ages.

Not Just a Social Trend

Given that our ideas around gender are socially constructed, some might argue that the current trend with an increase in youth identifying as transgender is a passing social phenomenon. Some might also argue that these youth are simply following a social trend. A few might even go so far as to say that kids are being pressured socially to identify as transgender.

And yet. It's almost always the other way around.

If anything, most gender-diverse youth feel social pressure to adhere to their assigned sex at birth. Teens don't want to be different; they want to be and feel "normal." Many teens, when asked, say they would not have chosen to be gender diverse if given the choice. Considering the social and emotional cost for trans people in coming out and making the changes needed to live authentically, it is easy to see how unlikely it is that one would do so to please one's friends or be a part of some group at school.

So, how *do* we account for the undeniable increase of youth identifying as gender diverse? It goes back to culture.

We live in a time when information is readily available, and we can see people of all kinds via media and social media. Youth today are exposed to the idea of gender diversity. They see others who are gender diverse, and this provides them with a concept and vocabulary for understanding something that had previously been confusing and amorphous. Many teens describe a "nagging feeling that something was off" or "a sense that I was not quite right." These same teens report that when they learned about gender diversity, their thoughts and feelings suddenly made more sense to them.

Dr. Angela Kade Goepferd is a pediatrician who specializes in the care and treatment of gender-diverse kids in Minneapolis. In her October 26, 2020 TED Talk, Dr. Goepferd eloquently explains that coming out as transgender requires "the words and the tools, the safety and the agency." Teens have access in our culture today to words that refer to and explain gender diversity. They have the tools to do their own research privately and at their own pace. They see gender-diverse role models and public figures and are discovering that being gender diverse is increasingly socially accepted.

There is no doubt that social acceptance drives "trends." Looking back at the 1920s, we see a similar trend involving handedness. Prior to 1920, it was considered wrong to be left-handed. Some thought it was a sign of the devil. Kids were punished for writing with their left hand. At the time, it seemed there were very few left-handed people because most of them were using their right hand, although it was not comfortable or most natural for them. Around 1920, the sentiment changed, and it was deemed silly to think that left-handedness was anything other than a natural occurrence.

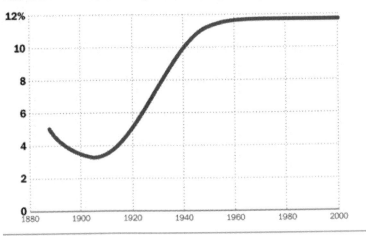

The history of left-handedness
Rate of left-handedness among Americans, by year of birth

WAPO.ST/**WONKBLOG**
Source: Survey data reported in "The History and Geography of Human Handedness" (2009)

It's quite possible that the same phenomenon is happening today with gender diversity. Scientists have gone on record declaring that there is no biological basis for a gender binary. In the words of Dr. Geopherd, our youth now have "the words and the tools." And when they feel safe and develop the agency, they claim their truth.

The Role of the Pandemic
Many teens came out as trans during the COVID-19 pandemic. There are different guesses as to why this occurred. The loudest explanation seems

to be that teens got caught up in social media and that it seemed "trendy" to come out as trans. But as just discussed, it has never been trendy or popular to be trans in Western culture, and teens know that coming out involves risking stigma and rejection and being subject to many social challenges.

The pandemic offered us a new perspective. It forced us to question what was most important in our lives. Adults reconnected with friends and family, left unsatisfying jobs, and rediscovered hobbies, faith, and the willingness to slow down. With death all around, many adults took stock of how they were living. They asked themselves if they were living according to their true values, doing what they genuinely wanted, and fulfilling their purpose or dreams.

And guess what? Teens did the same. They spent time alone. They thought about their lives. They reconnected to themselves and had time to consider what really mattered most to them. They were away from the daily peer pressures and societal expectations. And they had a chance to consider their own life path and contemplate what would feel most authentic and meaningful for them.

What many teens report is that the pandemic created a safe space for them to be away from the influence of school and peers and to be with themselves without distraction. It removed the daily pressure to conform that kids felt at school. It put a pause on all the gendered assumptions that bombard a teen daily at school. And it also gave them a chance to be alone with their thoughts and to explore topics they may have ignored during the rush of school. Many teens report the pandemic gave them time and space to explore feelings that had been lurking beneath the surface or acknowledge a deep knowing that their true gender identity differed from their gender assigned at birth.

Thoughts of mortality force us to reckon aspects of life we try otherwise to ignore. Thoughts of mortality embolden us to take risks we might otherwise have delayed in less severe circumstances.

Thoughts from a Therapist ...

I was working with a young adult who had been out as non-binary since they were thirteen. They were in college, earning a degree. They had friends and were dating. They seemed quite content in their life. When the pandemic hit, they took a semester off from college. While they were at home, they announced to their parents and our group that they had decided they wanted to get top surgery. The pandemic had forced them to consider their own mortality and the "thought of lying in a coffin with breasts horrified" them.

The Biology of Gender Diversity

Although outdated and oversimplified, most people are led to believe that the sex of a newborn is determined by the presence of either an XX chromosome pair (a baby girl) or an XY chromosome pair (a baby boy). However, science has advanced exponentially over the last several decades, and we now know that one's biological sex develops through the interplay of more than sex chromosomes alone.

For the first six weeks of pregnancy, we all start out with the potential to develop *either* testicles or labia. You could even say that a baby is essentially a small human without a biological sex at this point. At around six weeks into pregnancy, the development of the baby's biological sex is set in motion. Most fetuses, but not all, with an XX chromosome pair will develop ovaries, a uterus, and a vagina. Most fetuses, but not all, with an XY pair will develop a prostate, scrotum, and penis. In other words, while X and Y chromosomes are integral to this process, they do not, and cannot, singularly define one's biological sex.

For one thing, we now know that nature allows for variation in both the number and combination of sex chromosomes. That is, while most people have only two sex chromosomes, nature allows for some to have three chromosomes (e.g., XXX, XYY, or XXY) or even just one (e.g., X or Y).

In addition, though the genes on the Y chromosome will *generally* result in the development of male genitalia, they do not *always* result in the development of male genitalia. The process revolves around the activity of a particular gene, known as the SRY gene. The proteins produced by the SRY gene trigger the process to develop what we think of as "male" sex characteristics, such as a prostate, scrotum, and penis. However, the SRY gene doesn't always produce a functional protein and is also known to either "fall off" the Y chromosome or migrate to an X chromosome. In any of these cases, the process to develop male genitalia will not be triggered, in which case ovaries, a uterus, and a vagina will form despite the baby having a Y chromosome.

Another interesting insight that science has delivered in the last ten years is that biological sex and gender identity develop in different areas of the fetus and at different times during pregnancy. As just described above, the physical development and sexual differentiation of genitalia occur in the *first* trimester. However, a large bulk of brain development occurs in the *second* trimester, including the area of the brain that is primarily responsible for our deep internal sense of self and gender identity.

In other words, our biological sex develops during the *first* trimester according to *one* incredibly complex and layered process, and our gender identity develops in the *second* trimester according to *another* incredibly complex process.

For the majority of people (think bell curve), these two processes result in a biological sex and gender identity that match. However, through normal human variation, others will be born with the biological sex of one gender and gender identity of another.

Most of this normal variation goes unnoticed unless DNA tests or other medical inquiries are made to identify one's sex chromosomes. In the meantime, babies are born and assigned a biological sex based on physical attributes alone.

Have you ever wondered whether we are primarily driven by our biological sex or gender identity? The advent of structural magnetic resonance imaging (SMRI) has allowed studies to be conducted that suggest our brain overrides our body. For trans persons, SMRI scans show brain structure and activity more similar to their gender identity than to the sex they were assigned at birth.

Science will continue to evolve and may one day answer more of the questions still unanswered. For now, the idea of two X chromosomes or an X and a Y chromosome is oversimplified. How we emerge with the body and brain that we do is an immensely complicated and miraculous process in which a host of variations can result.

Sex (Re) Education

THE SCIENCE OF MANY SUBJECTS has changed since I graduated high school thirty years ago. Pluto lost its status as a full-fledged planet, indigo ended its masquerade as a primary color of the rainbow, and the biology of sex revealed itself to be far more complicated than XX and XY alone. Public school brought my son up to date on the first two but left him in the dark about the third. That one he had to figure out on his own, and along the way, I had to reeducate myself.

I know now that my son was in middle school when he first began feeling dissonance with, and distress about, his assigned gender. Maybe it existed as a formless idea in the recesses of his psyche before that; maybe not. I'll never know. What I do know is that as his body began taking on new contours, so did a grow-ing sense of gender dysphoria that he kept to himself. From my vantage point, on the outside looking in, I saw what I expected to see: a pubescent girl with an elevated amount of self-conscious-ness that I assumed would taper off in due time.

It took several years for my son to reconcile his post-puberty bodily discomfort and psychological pain with what his brain knew all along—that he was a boy in a girl's body. Along the way,

55

he went through hell. He tried starving his body to straighten and flatten his new curves. When that didn't work, he began living in oversized hoodie sweatshirts to obscure his chest. And when that still wasn't enough to relieve his distress, he cut his flesh with scissors that he hid in his room to bring the emotional pain into the physical realm, if only for a few seconds. Finally, a few weeks before he began his senior year of high school, he came out as a transgender male.

Initially, I avoided the planetary shift of his announcement. Though eager to *finally* have an answer to the years of his blind suffering, my mind scrambled. How could I have missed the signs? I was his mother, and given his mental health challenges, a hyper-vigilant one at that. And even if *I* had somehow missed the signs, wouldn't a doctor, therapist, or other specialist have seen them? I also worried that he might be attaching to the *idea* of being transgender as wishful thinking for an answer—any answer. I had no religious dogma in my way, only the long-held memory of XX and XY chromosomes from high school biology class and memories of him dancing around the house in princess dresses as a young child. Cinderella was his favorite.

The truth is that science is messy. Though we presume that "science" has the final say, it turns out that our scientific understanding of any given topic represents only the best hypothesis *available so far*. Technology changes, more information becomes available, and "science" changes—even if it takes years or decades for this new scientific understanding to be widely known and taught.

Case in point: my science teachers taught us that gender comes down to two "sex" chromosomes (XX=girl; XY=boy). Today, some thirty years later, the latest scientific understanding tells us otherwise. Thanks to advancements in modern genetic testing, scientists have uncovered a network of additional genetic, hormonal, and even cellular considerations at play. In short, we now know that someone born with a penis may actually have two X chromosomes. Likewise, someone born with a vagina can have an XY combo.

Science class also taught me to believe this was the complete story: the plumbing, the whole plumbing, and nothing but the plumbing. Again, science has evolved. It turns out that the brain plays an independent and equally leading role. Increasingly advanced and detailed brain imaging capabilities have allowed scientists to pinpoint our *felt* gender experience to specific areas within the brain. In other words, regardless of our plumbing, and no matter what other people want us to believe, we *are* the gender our brain tells us we are.

Unfortunately for me, however, I didn't yet have this more nuanced understanding of sex and gender when my son came out to me. In that gap, I struggled to make sense of what to think and what to do.

The cultural noise didn't help. Well-meaning friends and neighbors would ask me if I believed him; not-so well-meaning friends and neighbors told me he would "grow out of it." Over time, I came to see their knee-jerk responses as a luxury of the uninitiated—the luxury of having emotional distance from this deeply personal situation, and most likely the luxury of having their assigned gender match their plumbing and brain.

Because here's the thing: how can any of us say with any degree of certainty what it feels like to be someone else? And without that intimate knowledge, what right do we have to judge others' subjective experiences?

And so, I committed to honoring my son's subjective experience *and* to reeducating myself. I signed up for a parent series put on by a local therapist, watched videos on YouTube, and read articles. Lots of articles. Some articles were clearly biased one way or another; some were beyond my comprehension, and still others downright confusing. Still, I learned what I could, including the difference between gender identity (what we are) and gender expression (what we show) and that many species in the animal kingdom are transgender, including several types of fish capable of changing gender midlife. I also learned that out of the one hundred genes on the Y chromosome, only one (yep, just one!) determines the plumbing, and that this lone gene can (and does) sometimes fall off the Y chromosome or migrate to the X chromosome. When that happens, a penis can't and won't grow ... no matter how loudly a brain might wish for one.

My son is now twenty-one and traveling his unique, nonlinear path toward authenticity. Based on what I have learned, I try to hold lightly any preconceived notions I still have. Instead, I strive to see him as the miraculous universe of knowns and unknowns that he is.

Poignantly, parenting and supporting my son over the last several years has made me realize that we only see what we look for. Yes, he loved to wear princess dresses, play with Barbies, and wear makeup. But apply a different lens, and I also see that he loved Thomas the Tank Engine, idolized Percy Jackson, and insisted on wearing a necktie to his fourth-grade band concert.

In short, the fact that my son is transgender is the least interesting or radical thing about him. More remarkable is his deep empathy for others, his insanely imaginative and artistic brain, and his playful, inclusive, loyal, and sunny personality. And with or without science, he is due the same love, respect, and the freedom to live as his true self as any of us.

—Chrissy Boylan

My Emerging Queerness

I PROUDLY DISPLAYED my drawing of my family—my mom, my dad, and me—for the entire kindergarten class to see. Technically, my family was my dad and me at one house, and my mom, her girlfriend, and her girlfriend's son (my sort-of brother) at the other. But, only a couple months into my first year of school, I already had learned—from classmates asking their mom and dad if we could hang out after school and the excited discussions about this winter's father-daughter dance—that it was easier for my classmates to understand a family that looked like theirs. My teacher ushered us into our next activity, announcing it would be boys against girls. I followed all my other classmates with long hair and pink shirts to the left side of the room, where a sign of a stick figure in a pink dress was displayed.

That was my life for my first twelve years: barraged with constant messaging by society about what my family should look like, what I should look like, what my interests should be, how I should dress, and who I should love. I never thought to question it. I behaved like a "girly girl," as my family often affectionately called me. I loved dolls, puffy dresses, princesses, and all things pink. I had crushes on boys and acted shy and "ladylike." Yet, looking back, I often wonder whether *my* interests were really my own or rather a product of repeated messaging from society about how to fit in.

I first consciously questioned my identity in middle school, when I went to a camp for kids with LGBTQ+ parents on the shores of Provincetown. I was given the same assignment as I had in kindergarten—to draw my family. But, this time, I watched as my peers proudly presented colorful drawings of themselves holding hands with their two dads, their trans parent, or their three moms. So, I drew my mom and her girlfriend on one side of me and my dad on the other. At that moment, I realized it was *okay* that my family looked like that and that it would be okay if one day, many years later, my kid drew a picture of their family in their kindergarten class that wasn't a mom and a dad standing next to them. It would be okay if my kid had two moms. It would be okay if my kid had a parent who wasn't a girl *or* a boy. Maybe I didn't have to marry a man to be my kid's dad, and maybe *I* didn't have to be *a mom*.

Over the next few years, I began to allow myself to think more deeply about my identity. Did I really like that boy or was I just playing along since all my other friends seemed to like boys? Did I like my best friend as a friend or did I like her romantically? Was I just dressing how all the popular girls dressed? What clothes did *I* like? How did *I* want to express myself?

By junior year of high school, I thought I finally had settled into my identity as a lesbian. Then I found myself in the midst of a global pandemic, with the seclusion to experiment with my gender and a community of people online doing the same, without undesired feedback from society. I found that the online transgender communities I interacted with instilled this sense of resilience within me and were a significant aspect in my journey of understanding my identity. In 2020, I spent my days watching TikTok creators talk about their experiences with dysphoria and going on testosterone. I spent my nights alone in my room, waiting for my family to fall asleep so I could pin up my hair to make it look short and bind my chest without anyone knowing.

After a year of experimenting privately with my gender identity and expression, I decided the label "non-binary" and pronouns "they/them" felt right to me. As I got more confident in my identity, being referred to as "she" by my friends and family started to feel more and more like a slap in the face. So, I came out in hopes of feeling like myself again. First, to my friends, who all supported me. Then, with their support, I came out to my parents. As my mom held me and reassured me that she loved me no matter what, I felt for the thousands of kids kicked out of their homes for having been born in the wrong body. With my parents and my friends continuing to love me for who I am, I decided to devote my future to supporting those who don't receive that unconditional love.

I surrounded myself with the trans and queer community in every aspect of my life. I began working at the Boston Alliance of LGBTQ+ Youth, providing health education and risk reduction work to queer youth. I worked at a queer summer camp, living with and being a role model for trans and non-binary youth. And when I started college, I finally was able to explore my gender identity surrounded by friends who had only ever known me as non-binary. Being a role model, educator, and queer adult existing in the lives of queer youth I work with feels like something I want to do for the rest of my life and has greatly influenced my education choices, career aspirations, and current employment.

Now, over two years after initially coming out as non-binary, I find myself still routinely having to re-come out and explain my identity to those in my life. I hadn't anticipated having to answer my extended family's relentless questioning about my identity at every family gathering, or correct my parents for continuing to use the wrong pronouns over two years later, or decide if it's worth coming out to the doctor, server, or random person on the street so they'll stop misgendering me.

I also find myself continuing to come out, question, and experiment with my gender and explore how my gender intersects with other aspects of my identity. I've realized the importance of fluidity of identity: It's okay to continue to change and experiment, and that experimentation doesn't undermine or invalidate my identity. I'm so glad I've been able to find community and such positive queer spaces, and I hope to be able to continue to create these spaces for myself and others.

—Tia Sky

The Gift of Uncertainty

"SO, I WOULD SAY THERE'S ABOUT an 80 percent chance that you have a baby girl."

My husband and I had debated for days prior to the ultrasound as to whether we wanted to know the sex of our baby; we never considered the possibility of a less-than-certain answer. I would like to say the debate had been the result of us having a progressive view of gender, but as I recall, the debate was more about the surprise. Did we want to keep the big reveal for the delivery and, as an added bonus, be able to stave off questions about name and decor in the interim? I dreaded the idea of a wardrobe full of pink or blue clothes and then the baby being the opposite sex. Yet, if I were really forward thinking, what's wrong with a boy being dressed in pink or a girl being dressed in blue?

Many would say 80 percent certainty was a good indication that we were having a girl, but I was still stifled by that 20 percent. We decided to forego telling everyone that it was "majority" girl and declared the sex unknown. Progressive or not, I was somewhat relieved that we didn't become buried in pink even if we had a girl. Fortunately, the uncertainty led us to a classic Pooh decor that worked for both our firstborn (who five months later was assigned female at birth) and their little brother. That's the beautiful thing about classic Pooh; it's universal, unconditional love.

We seemed to understand gender stereotypes back then, but now why is the world of our non-binary sixteen-year-old so difficult to understand? I remember Austen telling us they had something they wanted to show us. It was a PowerPoint presentation that began with, "What is my favorite fluid?" They really liked science, so there was part of me that thought, *Perhaps this is about a state of matter somehow?* But then the next slide revealed "gender fluid." In fairness, my husband and I had been given hints. During COVID, at Austen's recommendation, we had spent many hours watching She-Ra episodes and Hallmark movies depicting positive lesbian relationships. We knew Austen might be trying to tell us something, but I must admit, the "gender fluid" designation was a bit of a conundrum. What did gender fluid even mean?

The presentation went on to say that Austen wanted to change their name officially at school (the main reason they were sharing, as we would need to sign the form). I know the name change can be hard, but for some reason, that was the least of it for me. While it was the name we had always called them, and the nickname was sentimental as it was my dad's, it was also just a name. They had put thought into their chosen name. They knew their middle name had been "Jane" as a tribute to Jane Austen, so they went with "Austen." For me, it meant a lot that they had tried to keep something of what we intended and made it their own.

There was a part of me that felt I could handle anything. If they were a lesbian or a trans male, okay, we would get more information and start a transition process, be it social or medical. But that's not how it worked for us. The name switch was for school, but Austen didn't want all the family to know. We stuck to that for some time, and my husband and I did the code-switching, but it wasn't so easy for their autistic little brother, who accepted "Austen" without question or judgment. However, he also couldn't call Austen by any other name, so they were outed by default whenever he was around.

While I embraced the name, I had a harder time with the fluid part. Some days, Austen wanted to wear bikinis and skirts, other days, chest binders and men's shorts. As much as I wanted to be open-minded and accepting, I wasn't prepared for not know-ing exactly what I was accepting. Uncertainty is hard for me. It's uncomfortable.

But why? I'll admit that I had previously embraced the comfort and certainty of conservatism. I was a Reagan Republican at ten and a confirmed Catholic at fourteen. I believed in a world of moral absolutes and grew up to have a church wedding with a full Mass. But for all the certain answers I sought, I also found contradictions. My Irish Catholic mother no longer went to church and instead read New Age books. A cousin who was like a sister to me also happened to be homosexual. I grew up seeing how she answered every slight and judgment with only unconditional compassion. She had so many heartbreaking relationships, and yet her generosity and forgiveness were unwavering. She lived a morality based on human kindness, not absolutes. Then I became a mother and realized that no one can prepare you for what your children will teach you about the world and how you see it.

As Austen socially transitioned, we became aware of the challenges that gender-diverse children face: the conservative religious relatives who you avoid telling for fear of disapproval and rejection, the opportunistic politicians who get elected by targeting your children to appeal to an intolerant base, and the misinformed friends and neighbors who start avoiding you as if trans is contagious. We have also faced the mental health battles that come with the depression and anxiety of feeling alone.

Uncertainty is uncomfortable. But what if we embraced uncertainty as a gift and a chance for exploration? Given the US divorce rate of 35 to 50 percent for first marriages (60 to 70 percent for second marriages), maybe we should avoid defining what constitutes an ideal relationship. And perhaps we should also reconsider why keeping a name assigned at birth is so important when nearly 70 percent of US women change their last name when they marry.

Even though I may not completely understand gender fluid, I do understand compassion. I have learned so much from Austen. Their courage in facing their own uncertainty and rejecting stereotypes of the binary world that surrounds them has taught me what it is to be simply human. What if we stopped feeling threatened by differences and instead embraced them?

If the world was made up of only ones and zeros, how would we explain the miraculous variation in hair, skin, and eye color that makes each of us unique? Or the testimony that Congress recently heard on unidentified organic material that is likely from an extraterrestrial source? If we can embrace the existence of variations and unknowns in the universe, then why can't we also embrace the unknowns in each other?

I remember holding Austen as a baby and understanding they were a miracle. Nothing in that understanding changes with their gender identity. I am grateful for the exceptional human being Austen continues to be. Would it be easier if they were simply an angsty teenager and gender fluid never entered our world? Is any teenager simple? Should our children ever be reduced to labels or trends instead of seen as humans, growing, learning, and doing the best they can? Perhaps they are all simply seeking the truth and understanding every one of us needs. And while this path looks different for trans kids, all of us will get there some day.

"Rivers know this: there is no hurry.
We shall get there some day."
Winnie the Pooh—A.A. Wilne

—Lisa

Staying Alive

I DON'T THINK I EVER CAME OUT to my parents. Instead, someone started a rumor in church that I liked girls. It was 2004, and I was fourteen going on fifteen.

I was dating a boy at the time, a punk kid with a mohawk and a beard. I thought the rumor was silly at first, a game played by my friends. I didn't think I displayed any behavior that would clue my peers into the questions going on inside.

Church was a multiple-day-a-week affair. Sunday, Wednesday, and Friday for service, and every other Thursday for counseling because my mother refused to take me to an actual therapist. I had gone through multiple traumatic events over that past year ... my grandfather's passing, sexual abuse from a close adult in my life, and my father who walked out on us again. I had also started another new school and was feeling displaced. All the kids had long-standing groups of friends, kids that had laughed and cried together since the wee days of elementary school. I did not. I had friends, sure, but I was still an outsider.

When the rumor started, my parents joined in on the teasing. Though maybe "playful" to their minds, I got mad and told them I was hurt. Instead of easing up, the velocity and ferocity only increased. I was shamed, blamed, ridiculed, and told that what I was "doing" was against God ... despite the fact that I wasn't doing anything. While my mom's teasing was only verbal, my sister used to hit me from time to time, make jokes about me being "mannish and fugly," and also joked about how it would be better for me to be a lesbian because if I had kids, they would be ugly.

My father was the worst, though, because he was far more crass and open-mouthed than my mom or sister. We used to bake cookies when we stayed with him. One night, he came out from the kitchenette with a tube of cookie dough he'd shaped into a penis and started yelling to me that "this is what dick looks like, see, they're great!"

One night after my Thursday counseling session at church, the youth pastor sent me home with a letter for my family. I thought it was either a prayer or a permission slip for one of the outings planned for the summer. Oh, was I wrong. It was a request for me to stop going to services because my "lifestyle" made the other girls uncomfortable. If I wanted to continue going or partaking in summer programs, the letter read, I would need to submit a written apology and denounce my "wicked ways."

I did not go back to that church.

I have known that I was a queer person since I was small, just without the vocabulary to encompass the experience. Later, in my early twenties, I came out to my friends as bi and then pansexual. I came out to everyone several years later and have been living openly as non-binary/agender ever since. I embraced living as my true self once my son and I finally got away from my ex-husband, who, once an anarchist, has unfortunately turned to the dark ways of Alex Jones and beyond.

After I left my ex-husband and got my license, I started dating my current partner, one of the first people I came out to long before we started dating. He encouraged me from day one to just be myself, whatever and whoever that meant. While I was figuring myself out and going through so many questions, tears, happiness, elation, and mourning, he was always patient and kind. He gave me such courage, and that courage has helped so much when parenting our son.

About five years after I came out as non-binary, my eleven-year-old son came out as trans. He was scared that being himself would hurt me because he wasn't "the same as before." I told him it was okay, that I had started piecing things together on my own, and that I was excited for him to get to be himself, finally. We cried a lot.

When he was little, he hated the way my parents only bought him pink, super femme things for holidays. He began to hate when his hair would get put up and having to present, mask, and validate my parents' obsession with his femininity.

He also always hated his birth name, especially the way my parents and grandmother would say it. It oftentimes seemed like they were jeering at him, but as a biblical name, their emphasis reflected their religious obsession with femininity. Outwardly, it sounded all singsong and jovial, but we didn't realize how triggering the name was for him. He apologized for that too. I told him that when I gave him that name, it was a gift and a blessing for his future, but that sometimes we outgrow gifts and no longer need them.

He kept his middle name.

We began to move into this new life with him and got him talking to a school counselor. We bought lots of gender-affirming clothes, new school supplies to match the aesthetic, books about being trans, and a bunch of library resources.

I had hoped that since he had love and support from both me and my partner, he would have an easier time at school and beyond than I did. I was wrong. Kids can be cruel.

Before he came out, they bullied him for being an emo kid, for not masking well enough, and for being too sensitive. He was into cool things, just not the same as everyone else. Now they bullied him for being trans.

By the final week of school, he made an unsuccessful attempt on his life.

He said he was sorry, that he just wanted some peace and quiet. I was devastated. We all were. It was one of the scariest moments of my life, and it felt like failure all across the board. I felt like a failure as a parent, and he felt like a failure at life because friendship is just so hard as a little guy. It's hard enough with math and puberty; it's even more so when you add bullying and teachers who protect the bully instead of the ones they hurt.

During this time, we learned that my partner's mother was extremely sick, a mixture of cancer, COVID-19, and arterial issues. She said she was dying, so my partner and I thought we should be with her in Indiana, to help get her affairs in order and foster a relationship between her and my kiddo before it was too late. It seemed like the blessing we needed, a fresh and safe start.

My son didn't want to go. He didn't want to leave his few friends or my family behind. I had my own trepidations based on previous experiences with her but wanted to do the right thing. I thought maybe my own mom-trauma was giving me wet feet, despite previous run-ins.

My son's depression grew as the time neared, and he started reaching out to my mom. She was subtle, but awful, twisting words about how I influenced the situation, how he's too young to mess up his body "like that." The conversations between them went on for a while and only escalated until he blocked her. He was so mad that she said such horrible things and couldn't understand that he just wanted to be happy and not feel bad about himself all the time.

When we finally moved, it was chaos. My partner's mother wasn't even there. She took a trip to Mexico and "forgot" to leave a note about where she left the keys. She ended up being gone for two weeks and left no way for us to get ahold of her. We spent all of our savings just trying not to be homeless. When she returned, she was mad that we didn't find the keys and even more mad that we waited to tell her about our son coming out.

She was a nurse, so I thought that her medical expertise gave her some greater know-how into parenting our son. At first, she tried to be nice but had a lot of unresolved issues with my partner, and our son got the brunt of her misplaced anger and frustration. She was extremely offended that our son didn't want to talk to her about menstruation and puberty, and she never made an effort to use his proper pronouns. Without cause, she even implied that he might be trans because he had been sexually abused as a baby. It was not the reason, and no, my boy was never abused.

After that, our son shrank away and tried to spend as little time with her as possible. She took huge offense, saying he was a psycho, that he was forcing himself to be depressed, and that it was an act. It felt like déjà vu, like being stuck in the same nightmare pattern again.

My partner and I fought with her over this, but it was *her* house. After three months of going around this terrible spiral, she kicked us out. On Christmas Eve. She threw our presents out in the snow and gave us an itemized bill of all the stuff she said we owed her, stuff she had bought for him, etc.

About a week after we got kicked out, I lost my job as a barista at a small coffee shop for being openly queer. I was devastated. We found a house and were able to move in shortly after, but living in a small hotel room for a month definitely messed with our morale. Somehow, we made it through though. Since then, we have removed our son from public school and have been home-schooling him with a more inclusive curriculum.

My son is a loving and caring individual. He is a skilled reader and debater. He loves art and is constantly exploring new medi-ums. He loves going to the library and taking part in the youth programs. He researches causes that are meaningful to him and sometimes scary. And he keeps trying to make new friends, even though he has been betrayed by so many people he held dear. I wish things didn't hurt him so much, but he has such a big heart.

We thought our time in Indiana was only going to be for a few months, but what was supposed to be a short-term engagement went horribly wrong, and our stay has been extended significantly. As I sit and write this, we are still trying to leave Indiana.

Living in Indiana is getting progressively more difficult. Our community here is small. We are trying to move back toward home on the East Coast, somewhere he can thrive, not merely stay alive.

Our son turned thirteen this year, and he is already braver than I will ever be, more empathetic and compassionate too. When he grows up, he wants to work with kids, either as a social worker or librarian. He just wants the chance to get there, to be himself in the process, something I relate to in a big way, and something I'm still learning to do myself.

My family was so unsupportive of my queerness that I ran away and lived on the streets from seventeen until the time my son was born. Everything I have learned was from trying to stay safe, to make a way for myself. I missed out on learning so many valuable life skills until I was an adult and realized that I deserved to know how to take care of myself and him. Because, by and large, we not only deserve the care and sensitivity, but we deserve the right to go places in life. Both physically and metaphorically speaking, we deserve the chance to be happy and successful. He makes me want to get better at doing that.

My heart hurts for all he's endured. I wish decisions I made in good faith had turned out better, but in so many instances, it truly seemed like the odds were stacked against us. Time after time, we kept on being disappointed, but I am also filled with hope, pride, and genuine love for him. I hope that Indiana legislation will stop terrorizing LGBTQIA+ people and that he and I both can live in a more inclusive environment. He deserves to walk down the street and not have people shout homophobic slurs at him.

I hope other people will meet him and see those things too, someday. Until then, I'm going to own my story. I'm going to continue telling people that trans people have the right to exist in our own beautifully diverse ways. I'm not going to back down because I love my family and am grateful for the lessons of compassion and empathy they teach me.

—**Bear**

Redacted

Being transgender is [REDACTED]
My pronouns are [REDACTED]
My age is [REDACTED]
I am [REDACTED], I am [REDACTED], get used to it.
My gender identity is [REDACTED]
I present [REDACTED]
I want [REDACTED] and [REDACTED]
But I am still [REDACTED], just like you.
Being cis and being trans aren't so different.
We all need [REDACTED]

—Lee

Coming Out

Just Embrace

We say,
be true,
be real.
So, let's see that truth
and read what's real.
What medicine and science reveal.
Don't get stuck in the past.
Be realistic.
Prevent the anguish of another statistic.
Winter, spring, summer and fall
Catch their tears when they fall
after a rain.
Refrain,
from causing pain.

Just embrace

Excerpt taken from *Just Embrace* by Rula Sinara

THE COLLOQUIAL TERM "COMING OUT" is appropriate because it underscores the fact that a person who has been having an internal experience is ready to share that internal experience by coming out with it.

The typical teen who comes out has grown up with exposure to gender diversity and may have been comfortable and knowledgeable on the subject even before they identified as trans. They have likely done months or years of research, have tried to deny their truth, and have finally come to accept themselves as gender diverse. They are ready to tell people and to choose a new name that suits them better than the one they were given at birth. They are ready to have their parents and friends use new pronouns in referring to them. And they generally know a fair amount about the trans community, being transgender, and what it is they envision for their future transition.

Coming out is a highly personalized experience and is often based on many forces in a teen's life, both tangible and intangible. Many teens choose to come out to their peers first, as was the case in our online survey. Seventy-seven percent of recipients reported that they came out to friends first. Others told a sibling, parent, or other trusted adult first. However, it matters less who they tell first than that they are ready to navigate the process. In other words, there is no right or wrong way to come out. The focus is better placed on the person coming out rather than any feelings about the who, how, and when.

PARENT(S) 10%

OTHER 2%

SIBLING 11%

FRIEND(S) 77%

To One's Self

Coming out to one's self can be a long and troubling process. As mentioned earlier, most teens explore their gender alone and in private, with the use of the internet, books, and online communities. This important stage of exploration might contain shame, confusion, and fear. Ultimately the exploration leads to a growing sense of one's gender identity and a coming out to one's self. Some teens might be eager to come out to select others (close friends or trusted family) upon realizing their gender identity. However, it is not unusual for some to wait until they develop a stronger sense of certainty, have the support of a therapist or online friends, and feel increased confidence in sharing this new discovery with others.

> **If you are a teen:** Know that your journey and process is your own. Your discoveries of self are your own. Your gender identity can be something you choose to keep private or something you choose to share with others. Allow yourself to proceed at your own pace and in your own way.

To Parents

Regardless of how or when it happens, a parent of a gender-diverse youth will eventually be faced with the realities of their child coming out. These parents, no matter how progressive they may be in thinking or lifestyle, need time to adjust and process the new reality.

parent perspective

How did your child come out to you?

Some parents said it was gradual ...

- It was a process. First, she said she thought she was bisexual, then a lesbian, and then finally confided to us that she didn't feel like a girl on the inside.

- He wrote me a note at first that he was bi, then later said he was pan ... then eventually that he is a trans male ... and several months later his new preferred name.

- It wasn't one event; it took months and there was uncertainty about what they were actually feeling.

- Slowly. Started experimenting with makeup and clothes and eventually just told me.

- He had spent half a year exploring and discussing non-binary gender identity in the abstract.

- Little by little and most communication was via text.

- There were a million little ways she tried to get us to see who she was.

- They sprinkled information over a few years and then told me outright. We have had a lot of amazing conversations lying on the bed looking at the ceiling.

- Gradually. First by using all pronouns.

Other parents said it was more abrupt ...

- Diagnosis after attempted suicide.

- She came out at ten, saying her insides didn't match her outsides.

- In an email that they sent moments before they walked out the door to go to sleep-away camp for a week!

- He woke me up in the middle of the night and handed me a note.

- Changed his Instagram profile.

- She cryptically asked me to make her an appointment with an endocrinologist for HT (which I had to look up to even know what she was talking about). She said, "I don't want to talk about it, you can connect the dots."

- She asked for a trans flag and asked if I knew why she wanted one.

- He wrote his feelings down and had me read it.

- Very gently during dinner one evening.

- We had a long late-night conversation and he told me.

- Handwritten note left on my nightstand early on a Sunday morning.

- During a quiet conversation in the car.

Many parents will be unfamiliar with the concept of gender diversity until their kid comes out as trans. Even relatively "progressive" parents who support LGBTQ+ rights may not have previously known a trans person. They may not understand the science and culture of gender diversity and might still be rooted in the concept of the binary and conditioned to see their child as the sex assigned to them at birth. Naturally, they may be confused, upset, or scared and not at all ready to take steps forward. They need time to learn, process, and adjust.

Some parents delay the emotional journey by throwing themselves into the task of researching gender diversity. They may register for a class or workshop, read one or more books, talk to a therapist, or identify support services available for their teen. Hopefully, they are also lining up support for themselves.

Nevertheless, all parents will eventually have to contend with the host of emotions, conflicting and otherwise, that inevitably follow a child's coming out. There is no right or wrong way to feel, and parents will likely feel multiple emotions at various depths simultaneously. Here are some of the most common responses:

Surprise and Denial

Many parents are surprised when their teen comes out as transgender. Some report that it is entirely unexpected and seems to have "come out of the blue," and that they "never saw this coming." These parents sometimes turn to social media to connect with other surprised parents, where they hear reports of kids being influenced by social media and cling to a hope that this is a phase. Parents may wonder if their kid has been influenced by peers or simply doesn't like the changes brought about by puberty. What they don't know is that for their kid, this has likely been brewing for quite some time. Their kid may have been trying to play by the social rules, and they may have appeared to be comfortable conforming. Hiding their gender difference was intentional, and they might have done it well. So it makes sense that parents "didn't see this coming." That doesn't mean their child is confused, impulsive, or influenced by peers. It simply demonstrates the power of the social rules and expectations and a kid's effort to fit in and conform.

Fear and Anxiety

Parents are human. They live in the same society in which trans individuals are often maligned. They don't want their child to have a more challenging path than they would as a cisgendered person. They naturally hope that their child is "confused" or "being influenced by others" or "going through a phase of exploration." They anxiously wait for the phase to pass. When it doesn't, they begin to feel challenged with how to support their child while avoiding rash decisions.

Disbelief

When a child with a history of social and emotional challenges comes out as transgender, some parents are prone to think that this is "simply the latest challenge." It may take a while for them to realize that maybe the gender issue is at the root of the other concerns. Already invested in addressing the existing concerns, it is common for parents to remain on course and not shift their focus to the gender issue. For this reason, many teens report that they told their parents about their gender confusion and their parents "didn't do anything" or "didn't seem to believe me." Most of the time, this is not due to callousness or neglect. Parents honestly believe that the support in place will address all relevant concerns. However, gender support is rather specific, and unless it is being addressed directly, by someone specifically trained to do so, it often goes entirely unaddressed, even in therapy.

Grief

Upon learning that their child is not who they thought they were, many parents eventually find themselves going through the various stages of grief. And some report feeling guilty for doing so. However, grief is the process of coming to terms with anything that feels like a loss, and to many parents, learning their child is transgender includes a sense of loss. They have formed hopes and dreams for their children that started before the child was even born. When they first meet their newborn or adopted child, they begin a prolonged process of imagining that child's future. When the child discloses a gender incongruence, parents may have to let go of some of what they imagined. This leaves many parents feeling disoriented and uncertain.

As parents process grief and other emotions, many eventually come to a place of acceptance. Some parents find a sense of purpose and a deeper sense of their own humanity, even feeling gratitude for the experience that inspired it. These parents describe the strength they have gained as a family and appreciation for the community they have found. They celebrate their child's courage and their own deepening connection to their child. They report that the entire journey has been meaningful. Often these same parents serve as mentors, offering hope and encouragement as another parent travels the path from grief to gratitude.

In most families, the initial coming out stage is ripe with misunderstanding between parents and their gender-diverse youth. While youth often feel a sense of relief at having finally come out, parents are often in distress. While youth often feel knowledgeable and emboldened, parents feel confused and wary. Teens may be happier than they have been for some time, and parents might be grappling with sadness. At this point, many (even most) parents say things they later regret. They say things out of concern, ignorance, denial, or fear. To a teen who is asking for acceptance and support, these statements can be devastating and lead to feelings of hurt and anger.

Some teens will feel guilty that they have created distress for their parents and may try to retreat ... to stop their quest to move forward and assume their parents will "never support me." They may go back "in the closet" and return to trying to adhere to gender expectations. When they do this, parents eagerly assume this was "just a phase" or "an impulsive teen thing." Parents may be content to "just ignore it." However, true gender incongruence cannot be ignored forever. And ignoring it comes at a cost.

If you are a teen: Try to understand that even though your parents need time to adjust, it does not indicate their true feelings of support for you. You may find that once they have had time to learn and absorb it all, your parents become your biggest champion! A parent's need to grieve is about letting go of their own expectations, not letting go of you. These expectations are often embedded in the gender binary, have been culturally instilled, and have been held for a long time. Grieving is a way for parents to examine these conditioned expectations and realize that they are unfair and do not apply to you. Give them a little space; this is something they need to work through on their own.

If you are a parent: Try to understand that no teen shares this truth with a parent impulsively. This is not something that your teen came to accept easily, and it is most likely not a passing phase. Try to appreciate that your teen has fought a long and hard inner battle to get to the point of sharing their fragile truth with you. Understand that their drive to move forward is not hasty, and do your best to support their path in whatever ways you can. Try to understand that your emotional response is likely to cause your teen to feel guilty for having "put you through this" or angry that you cannot jump straight to "happy" acceptance.

While you are grappling with intense emotions, your child may be moving excitedly through stages of identity formation and fulfillment as they begin to actively live in their true gender identity. They are celebrating as you are grieving. This is a recipe for conflict. You are entitled to your emotions. Allowing yourself to feel them is your best path forward and is ultimately an act of love. But, like many things that parents contend with while raising kids, it is not something to share with your kid. Avoid statements like "I miss my little girl" or "I can't believe you are no longer my son." These statements may be a genuine reflection of your grief process but can be extremely hurtful to your child. Share your experience with your partner, friends, or therapist, but *not* with your child.

If you are a therapist: This is an extremely hard road to navigate. The teen deserves to be supported and celebrated. They need to be encouraged to claim their truth and begin to find their truest expression of self. But parents also deserve the time, safe space, education, and support *they* need. The two sometimes seem completely at odds with one another. Balancing these differing needs can be challenging.

Parents need a safe place to process their own emotions. Teens need to understand that their parents' grief is not an indicator of rejection. Teens benefit from learning that their parents are going through a process that will ultimately lead to acceptance. Teens need guidance in relinquishing any guilt they may have about being the source of their parents' anguish. Parents need to be supported in moving through this process without sharing it in detail with their child. No trans child should be asked to participate in their parent's grief process.

Credit is owed to Liz Schnelzer, LCSW, CCI, who contributed greatly to this segment by sharing her expertise on grief.

teen talk

What meaningful things did your parents do to support you on your gender journey?

- *Educating themselves on transgender topics: Taking the time to learn and understand the challenges and experiences of transgender individuals is a crucial step in providing support.*

- *Coming to terms with unconscious biases: Acknowledging and addressing any preconceived notions or biases they may have had, allowing them to better support you without judgment.*

- *Respecting my name and pronouns: Showing respect for my identity by using my preferred name and pronouns is a significant way to validate my identity.*

- *Changing my legal name: This demonstrates their commitment to fully recognizing my transition and ensuring my identity is legally protected.*

- *Allowing me to start masculinizing hormones at a young age under medical supervision: Supporting my medical transition under the guidance of a qualified doctor shows their dedication to my well-being and happiness.*

To Extended Family

Relationships with extended family and in-laws are often complicated, even before there is a trans family member. However, when a youth comes out as trans, relationships can get even more dicey. Many parents worry that the relationship their teen has with their grandparents will be adversely affected after the grandparents learn of their gender diversity. And, unfortunately, many of these parents are correct.

Their own parents, of an older and more conservative generation, are confused and upset by the notion of gender diversity. Many grandparents even criticize parents for "allowing this to happen." Comments such as these often cut deep for parents who are struggling to find the best response to their child's disclosure.

On the other hand, many families are pleasantly surprised to learn that grandparents, although they may not understand, are able to demonstrate unconditional love for their grandchild and offer support to the parent who is struggling.

Either way, ask a group of teens, "Whose acceptance do you most want and don't have?" and the likely answer will be "my grandparents."

If you are grandparent or extended family member: Please know that your love, support, and acceptance can make an enormous difference in the life of your young trans family member. Thank you for reading this book and educating yourself. Gender diversity might seem foreign to you and even unsettling, but once you talk to your younger family member, ask questions, and listen with an open mind, you will begin to see they are the same kid you have loved all along.

Thoughts from a Therapist ...

Every year in October and November, many of the teens I work with begin to worry about the upcoming holidays. Jane's experience encapsulates what many teens go through. Jane had come out as a trans female early in the summer and her parents had struggled to accept this. It was now early November, and they were "coming around." While they still made mistakes, her parents had begun using her new name and female pronouns.

The family tradition was to see one set of grandparents for Thanksgiving and the other for Christmas. Jane was distressed about what to do. She felt that neither she nor her parents were ready to share her trans identity with extended family. But not doing so meant assuming the role of a boy during the holidays. She couldn't bear the thought of having to wear men's attire and go by her old name. But she also couldn't imagine showing up as her true feminine self. Her parents understood her dilemma and tried to give her some choice in the matter. Part of Jane wanted to avoid the holiday interactions altogether, but she also loved her grandparents and enjoyed seeing her cousins. She didn't want her parents to have to miss out on the holiday events, and she knew they were not yet ready to explain her gender identity to the older generation.

At School

The school environment plays an enormous role in the life of a trans teen. For some, school is a haven, a place where friends use their chosen name and pronouns. These teens feel like they are able to be themselves at school, while at home, their parents are still adjusting to news of their gender identity. They can meet other gender-diverse teens, form supportive friendship circles, join clubs, and thrive in the school environment. For them, school is a respite since at home they might feel less supported and embraced.

For others, school is a dreaded nightmare where they are bullied or harassed, excluded, misgendered, and afraid to use the restroom. For some, the most they can hope for is to go unnoticed. Some kids refuse to attend school due to constant bullying. Parents who have the means may opt to place them in a smaller, more supportive school environment. Many students assess their school environment and determine it is not safe to come out. They deliberately hide their true identity until they graduate high school. It is absolutely impossible for any student living with that kind of distress to do their best in school.

For the most part, school has been and continues to be a tenuous place for trans teens. Most teachers have no training, formal or otherwise, on how to show support to trans students. In addition, despite the social dysphoria and mental distress associated, most schools lack a protocol for students or parents to request usage of preferred names and pronouns.

In some areas of the country, teens have started speaking up on their own behalf and parents have begun advocating for their kids. In those areas, some school districts are listening, and teachers are receiving training in how to make trans students feel safe and respected.

Unfortunately, however, and depending on where you live, the school environment may have *regressed* in recent years. For example, in state legislatures all across the country in 2023, more than 300 anti-LGBTQ+

bills related to education were filed, a quarter of which were eventually signed into law. These bills attempt to restrict educator or student rights in various ways, including but not limited to:

- Forbidding use of name or pronouns inconsistent with biological sex on birth certificate
- Denying access to bathrooms or other school facilities that align with one's gender identity
- Restricting or censoring teachers altogether from discussing LGBTQ+ people and issues
- Banning transgender students from participating in sports consistent with their gender identity
- Requiring school staff to out transgender youth to their families, whether or not this puts a child at risk of harm

Though many of these policies are direct violations of several federal and state laws and will eventually be overturned in the courts, in the meantime, countless innocent kids are suffering the distress of feeling like their school environment is not safe. And their parents worry about their safety and mental health.

teen talk

What advice would you give school administrators about supporting trans and non-binary students in school?

- Lead, and others will follow. Create an accepting and welcoming environment, and let students know that there is nothing wrong with being genderqueer.

- A school environment where all kids can be themselves benefits everyone!

- Make sure teachers are educated about supporting trans students.

- Listen to the LGBTQ+ students about what they want.

- Be open to new perspectives and understand how "life and death" it can be to support trans kids.

- Many trans kids do not have supportive or understanding families; school is a place where we can feel free and be ourselves with our friends.

- Having gender-neutral bathrooms available is a lifesaver.

- Have anti-bullying policies and actually enforce them. Empty words mean nothing, there needs to be follow-through.

- Please be kind and have empathy for what we are going through.

In the Community and Beyond

Rarely are all family members in agreement about when and who should be informed of the change in gender identity. Sometimes teens are reluctant, while parents are eager to tell their closest friends and family so they can receive support for themselves. Sometimes teens are ready to announce their truth, yet parents would prefer to wait. They may need more time to acclimate and feel prepared to answer questions that might come their way.

Negotiating when and who to come out to is a tricky process for most families. It is important that parents and teens communicate openly about this and work toward compromises everyone can feel comfortable with. It is helpful when teens grant their parents permission to tell their own closest confidants, and it is also important that parents respect the privacy of their teen and not disclose any information that has not been agreed upon.

It is important to note that many youths choose to tell trusted friends and family and *not* a wider circle of peers at school and extended family. This can be a challenging time for parents who must develop the skill of "code-switching"—moving back and forth between the child's given and chosen names, old and new pronouns—depending on who they are interacting with and whether their kid has come out to them.

Thoughts from a Therapist ...

The act of coming out takes tremendous courage. In the teen groups I facilitate, we celebrate each time a member comes out to someone new. The other teens understand and appreciate the bold move it is and the risk it takes to share one's truth with no guarantee it will be accepted and respected. Even after teens have been out for a while, and to most of the people in their life, each new person requires another surge of courage. Some teens report that it gets easier, but some say that it is terrifying every time.

Choosing Myself

I TRIED NOT TO THINK ABOUT IT all that much while growing up. I stayed within the bounds of gendered clothing sections and the closet full of things I only sort of liked on the best of days. I avoided looking in the mirror for too long, at least avoided *really* looking.

I didn't know what to do with my hair. I pulled it back and eventually cut it. Even that required months of convincing myself that it wasn't going to be the end of the world. My mom hated it; she told me I looked butch. People called me "brave" for doing it. I didn't know how I felt, but I knew that I couldn't go back. It meant something bigger, though, which I wouldn't let myself understand for a couple more years.

I wore school uniforms from fourth grade until I graduated high school. I loved them, even when they were uncomfortable and stuffy. I loved not having to think too hard about my place in the world, loved not having a choice in the matter. Choice wasn't *safe*, it wasn't easy, and I wanted nothing to do with it. How I looked, what I wore, who I was supposed to be was all laid out for me in a school handbook, and I followed it to the letter. It didn't make me happy, but it made me invisible. It made me safe.

It was easy, at first, to bury those feelings below when I realized how dangerous it was to feel the way I did. Easy to stay insulated and isolated inside my own skull, where nobody could see me, judge me, or form an opinion about me.

But there was a problem with my approach, my aspiration to be invisible, unobtrusive, and only in my own head—eventually, I couldn't keep it all contained. It was a war against myself, and I was losing. There were a million odd things I did, from the clothes I chose to wear outside school to the way I walked, talked, and gestured. Everything about me was out of alignment, out of focus, and I was sure that people could sense it, even when I said nothing or did nothing to warrant any attention at all. They knew, as well as I did, that something about me was *different*, and nothing I could do would change that.

All the while I drifted further and further from myself, from my future, and from the world around me. I detached. I buried myself before anyone else had the chance to do it for me.

Once, when I was sixteen, I threw my arms out in frustration as I argued with my mom. She gave me this sideways glance, her face painted with disgust, and said, "Stop gesturing like a man." I grew more heated, and I gestured again, bigger this time, as my pulse pounded in my ears. "What the hell does that even mean?" I replied. "That's *ridiculous*. That's the stupidest thing I've ever heard. *Gesture like a man*, how the hell else am I supposed to gesture?"

She rolled her eyes, and on we went arguing about nothing that would be worth remembering. But the fragment of that memory has clung to my mind. It felt like she had seen right through me and was disgusted by what she found.

Meanwhile, I was in denial. Enough that I had forgotten how two years earlier, after wearing ace bandages wrapped around my ribs for months and dressing in the closest things I owned to men's clothes, my dad asked, with a Christian therapist sitting across from us, if I really wanted to be a gross, stinky boy. I had forgotten the panic I felt when he told my mom and she asked me about it. I had forgotten how I told the therapist, "Actually, I think I'm just a lesbian, I don't think I'm a boy." As if I was solving the problem in one fell swoop, without having to suddenly become more visible to all the people who looked down on me. At least that would be something I could hide.

And I'd said to myself, before I buried it, that it wasn't that bad, that I was just convincing myself because I hated my own life and just needed to focus on bettering that first. I convinced myself that I could find a way to exist within the bounds I was assigned, as much as possible, even if it made me feel wrong and uncomfortable. It was *bearable,* and that would have to be good enough because the thought of needles scared me, and so did people knowing I was different and having everything change.

As much as I *wanted* everything to change, I wished for it in the way one wishes they had been born somebody else: as a nice thought to escape into, but wholly unreachable and not worth entertaining. Much like the pleasant and impossible idea of being born somebody else, I decided that having any amount of control over this piece of me was equally as fantastical, so I buried it, albeit ineffectually, and tried to be something that seemed easier.

But it wasn't.

And it never would be.

As much as I tried to be this odd, faded-out version of myself, I found it was almost impossible to maintain. Eventually, I would brush up against things that would aggravate that old wound, *reminding* me that something about the way I was experiencing gender was off. It made me scared to confront these feelings head-on, and so I wouldn't. Instead, those feelings sat there, buried deep inside, eating away at everything about me.

The older I got, the more complex my life became, the more it grew and dug itself out from its hiding place. And no matter how hard I tried, no matter how many caveats and compromises I tacked on by cutting my hair and deciding to just secretly identify as non-binary so I wouldn't have to tell anyone, I was still left with the same truth I had known my whole life: I was a man trying my hardest not to be, and it wasn't working.

It was a feeling that was eating me alive, a thing I refused to look at or acknowledge until I couldn't hide from myself anymore. I was incapable of not being myself, and to be myself was to be thrust from invisibility and safety into the maws of a world ready to tear me apart. Because when I was fourteen and denied what I knew to be true, I didn't suddenly feel any different. I had simply debated and bargained with myself and chose to ignore the future coming right for me until I was seventeen and facing the prospect of this being *the rest of my life.*

And that really snapped it all into focus; I was no one, going nowhere, with no real desires or dreams that I could craft for this person I was trying so hard and doing so badly at being. Maybe I had just assumed that I would blink out of existence at eighteen. After all, to my teenage brain, years were long, and adulthood was far, far away and amorphous. But it came up faster than I could have ever fathomed. And that's when I knew it was time. There was nowhere left to run.

Coming back to it wasn't happy, wasn't even relieving. It was a funeral march; it was turning around and facing the wolf I had been running from with nothing but my bare hands to protect me. I was seventeen, and I was dying inside and so terribly alone and scared. It was me asking my first boyfriend if he was going to leave me now because I wasn't what he signed up for when I came out as bisexual and told him I liked him too. It was standing in the men's section in the mall, trying to hide how my hands shook as I took pieces of men's clothes like it was illegal for me to even look at them. It was this weight that sat in my chest and this feeling that this thing I had ignored was going to kill me if I didn't deal with it now. I had my back against the wall, with nowhere to run. I had run out of compromises, out of excuses, and ways to avoid it.

It was time.

I had to choose to be scared.

Way more scared than when I cut my hair the day after my sixteenth birthday and tried to convince my mom it didn't mean anything.

Transition is one of those things where it feels like it takes forever in the moment, but then you blink, and it's six years later, and all your memories are fuzzy and far away. I think back, and most of my life feels like an odd fever dream I've just recently woken up from. I feel like I'm thinking about somebody else when I recall these feelings and what I went through to get here. But no, that was me. I lived all those moments, and I made it here, today; six years of choosing to be scared and having every second be worth it. Six years of big, impossible, wondrous change.

And it has changed *everything*, but it also hasn't. I still play the same video games, sometimes. I still listen to the same music. I still wear some of the shirts I got back in high school. I still talk to people from my childhood and adolescence. I still have that deep bond with the one friend from high school that I'm still close friends with. But me now? It's like I have been pulled up out of drowning and now I'm able to breathe again. Like I came into focus, gradually and then all at once. It's that wonderful feeling of having gone from surviving to really *living*. And that I wouldn't change for anything.

I still think about that kid, facing down this big scary thing, unable to ask for help or support. I still think of how I, at many points, was likely to not make it to eighteen. I think about the first year of my transition, when I was sitting across from my mom in a booth in a Mexican restaurant as she told me, "You know that no one will ever love you, right? You're not a real man." I think about how I have old friends and family I will never speak to or see again because they feel like everything I've done is wrong. And I can't change that.

My mom came around eventually, my life normalized, and I'd say that now I'm perfectly alright and happy with how everything has ended up. It's not what I wanted when I prayed to wake up a boy in the morning every week for months when I was five, but that's never been how reality works.

I have found my own happiness in spite of not being able to go back and live out my childhood and adolescence as a boy. But, man, if I could, I would have been a little boy and grown up how I really wanted to. Maybe that way everything about me wouldn't have been so wrong; maybe I would've been a bit more confident and outgoing and way less depressed. But more than anything, if I could change anything other than how I was born, I would have wanted my parents to have seen and supported me in being who I am from the beginning. I think that was harder than anything else.

Despite that, this life isn't so bad; I think of the people who have loved me and who do love me. I think about the mentors I've had, the community I've found. I think about all the people out there who are like me and have happy lives too. We love and are loved. We have families, chosen or otherwise. We raise children, and we lead communities. We have careers. We make art. We keep moving forward. We have to.

And, so, when I was on the verge of eighteen, I was presented with a choice: live as if I was already dead, knowing that the suffocating safety would ultimately kill me, or take a chance and step into the open and into all the things that scared me. Choosing to be scared was the hardest, most painful, and bravest thing I've ever done.

—Jackson

We Say

She says
Mom and Dad, I've got something to share
I've been thinking a lot, and it's just not fair
To hide from you who I know I've become
I was never your daughter; I was always your son

We say
You were born a girl, and that won't change
Don't tell us you aren't the daughter we've known
This whole idea is very strange
We named you as well, and we've seen how you've grown

She says
Those names are dead, and my pronouns are new
Respect me and honor my wishes please
The old ones don't fit, and they just don't do
Getting this far sure wasn't a breeze!

We say
We need time to grieve and we need time to mourn
We need time to research and we need time to learn
You tell us you aren't the child we've borne
You've had time to think, and now it's our turn

We Say

He says
I hear what you're saying, just don't let me down
I know this sounds easy, but it's hard not to drown
When I feel like my body just doesn't fit
It throws off my balance, my heart, and my wit

We all say
This odyssey's tough, but we'll come out okay
We'll support each other each step of the way
We'll get help to make it through day to day
And think twice when we have something to say

Some things will change, and some things will not
We've loved each other since you were a tot
Now we encounter a twist in our plot
Our daughter's our son—let's give this a shot

—Valerie Banks Amster

Crashing

WHEN MY KID WAS THREE, we moved to a Virginia suburb, and the first thing I did after I unpacked our boxes was sign up for a membership at the closest pool. I grew up near the beach, and the only time during my entire childhood I was not there or splashing in a pool was those thirty minutes after eating when you had to sit and wait. I wanted Alex to have a childhood spent in the water.

We had ten summers of after-dinner swims and weekends at our local pool, playing elaborate games that involved us being dolphins and my husband being a shark, or a zombie, or a zombie shark. We took vacations to my husband's family's lake house or the beach. Alex loved the water and sand as much as I did.

And then, just before Alex turned thirteen, it all changed. He started refusing to go to the pool. I'm too tired, he'd say, and it took cajoling and bribing to get him in the car, and then once we were there, he'd refuse to put on a suit.

And then there was the frustrating spring break in Florida. We'd gone to visit my husband's brother, and a five-minute drive from his house is Honeymoon Island State Park, this small barrier island in the Gulf. But getting Alex out of the car in the Honeymoon Island parking lot was a nightmare. We finally dragged him out to the beach where he slept all day, hidden under a bunch of towels, in his hoodie and sweatpants.

What had happened to my little fish? Everyone warned me that the teen years would be rough, but as the months passed, I realized we needed help. I found Alex a therapist, and after doing the hard work, one night, my child rose up out of the waves of that dark sea, and like Venus standing on that clamshell, revealed her true self to me.

My kiddo, assigned male at birth, was actually a girl, she explained. My first reaction was pure relief. Now we could both move forward—Alexis, as she now wanted to be known, growing into her authentic self and me growing into her biggest advocate and supporter.

I took on the job like it was a calling. I read books, joined groups, enlisted a whole team of professionals to help us. I explained things to teachers and family members. I learned a new vocabulary: dysmorphia, gender dysphoria, deadname. At my most aggressively optimistic, I found a company online, because you can find anything online, that specializes in swimwear for trans teenage girls, and I ordered a suit.

I was so focused on making sure Alexis felt totally supported that I never slowed down to consider how *I* was processing this momentous change. I love my kid—how can I be anything but 110 percent on board? And this isn't about me, right? It's about her.

Then, a full year into this journey, I crashed. I was at work, waiting for a Zoom meeting to start, when I glanced over at my phone. While it's charging, it plays a steady, random slideshow of photos from the cloud. I watched as it served up old photo after old photo of my adorable little boy. And each picture hit me with the force of an ocean wave. That little boy is gone. And so is the teenage boy I had hoped to guide into adulthood. Or the young man I had dreamed about dancing with at his wedding.

Intellectually, I know part of parenting is letting go as your child moves through stages, but this was letting go of too much. I felt sad and then, immediately, ashamed of myself. *I'm supposed to be happy that she's happy now, right? What's wrong with me?*

The feelings didn't go away. To Alexis, I kept being the advocate, the supporter, but I had this dirty little secret. It was always the photos that set me off. I couldn't look at one without tears welling up. I turned my phone face down to charge it. I spent months of whiplashing between, "Oh, you look so pretty, honey, I love that eye shadow on you," and feeling like I was going to lose it. I knew I couldn't keep this up.

A therapist we'd worked with said she was starting a six-session group for parents of transgender kids focused on coping with grief. *Well, it kind of makes sense, and six sessions, okay, not a lot, but if I put in the hard work, I'll graduate from Grief Class, and maybe that'll give me a reset.*

From the first session, it was total, judgment-free validation. Being sad is a perfectly reasonable reaction, the therapist said. You can love and support your kid 110 percent and still mourn the loss of the child you once knew. It's okay. Both of these things can be true.

Here's what else I learned in Grief Class. Those stages of grief we've all heard of—denial, anger, bargaining, depression, acceptance—they're not a linear progression. You don't check one off and move on to the next stage. The therapist said to think of it this way: Grief is a sea, and the stages are islands, and you're drifting, crashing into one island, then another one, again and again. But one day, you'll find yourself spending more time on the island of acceptance, and eventually, it can even be what she calls joyful acceptance.

The other thing I learned is that bargaining doesn't necessarily mean you try to strike some kind of deal with God—if I do this, you'll give me that. It's also obsessing over every moment you wish you'd done differently. *Why hadn't I been more compassionate when Alexis stopped swimming? If only I'd figured out her secret sooner.* That's bargaining, and it's the island I visited so often, you'd think I had a vacation home there.

I don't know if it was the therapist, or talking with the other parents, or just the permission to feel what I was feeling, but it all helped. There was no big a-ha moment, just a gentle drift. One day I caught myself looking at baby photos and I was smiling. Because this journey I'm on, this life, is freaking amazing.

THIS SPRING, WE WENT BACK to my brother-in-law's place in Florida. And as soon as we got there, Alexis said, "Mom, let's go to the beach. Just you and me."

Well, when your teenager actually asks to spend time with you, you do not say no. So, we jumped in the rental car, and I hot-footed it over to Honeymoon Island.

We parked in that same parking lot, where three years earlier, I could barely pull her out of the car. We got our towels and chairs out of the trunk, and then Alexis pulled off her hoodie and sweats and threw them in the backseat. She stood there in that swimsuit I'd ordered, that bikini, tossed back her hair, and said, "Look at us. Two hot babes at the beach."

I found us a spot, a few feet from where some teenage boys were tossing a football—yeah, I was a teenage girl once. I know how to pick a spot on the beach. I set up my chair, but Alexis set hers up about ten feet back so if one of those boys came by, she wouldn't look like she was with her mother.

I pulled out my phone and took a selfie, with Alexis in the background, oblivious to being in the shot, completely unself-conscious, reveling in an outer self that finally matched her inner self. I wriggled my toes in the sand and listened to the waves. I wasn't out there in the sea, crashing into islands of bargaining, or depression, or denial. I was with my daughter on Honeymoon Island, the island of joyful acceptance.

—B

Did I Disappoint You?

Did I disappoint you?
Did I let you down?
When I opened my mouth
And said what I needed to
Were you scared then?
Of who I'd become
Despite every effort to the contrary
I, your son
Am I a shame to you?
Born a wolf in sheep's clothing
As I walk a road you never wanted for me
I am meant for corners and closets
Binding, winding restraints
Of history and religion
I saw it in your eyes a million times
The disappointment and the shame
So speak up
Tell me the truth
Did I disappoint you?

—Jackson

The Runaway

FRIDAY NIGHT: I plot. This week, OUTMemphis announced a Trans Resource Fair on Instagram. As soon as I realize there will be free gender-affirming haircuts, I'm certain I will be there. I've never once gotten my hair cut before. Short hair has been in the back of my mind since I was little. My thick, long curls did not give me grief until my styles evolved from natural twists and pigtails to butterfly locs and cornrows into a high bun. My hair essentially marked my progression from "cutesy girl" to "young woman." In January, I kept glancing at my video on the screen of my Zoom class. With my face covered in makeup and hair in goddess braids down my back, I felt utterly disgusting. I logged off early, unable to stand the sight of my face for another second.

It is November 18, 2022. I can't drive, even though I am twenty years old. I also have no in-person friends and barely possess a cell phone. So, how will I get to the Resource Fair? I hope social media can pull me through. On Instagram, I spot a post tagged in Memphis, Tennessee. According to the profile, Lavender Sunshine is a non-binary Memphian. I nervously ask if they—or any of their friends—are interested in attending the fair. They reply, "Maybe. Need to check my schedule." It's 10:30 p.m., so I have to turn in my phone. In bed, I stare at the ceiling for ages. I hate feeling so unsure of what's to come.

SATURDAY MORNING: My mom enters my room to check her outfit in my full-length mirror. She's headed to a funeral, an unfortunate norm for her on Saturday mornings. However, it is somewhat fortunate for me because it means I have a better chance of making today's plan a reality. My dad's always been more easily persuaded than Mom. After she leaves, I hurry to her bedroom to grab my phone. Yes! They confirmed they're willing to take me today! I shoot them my address and a good time for pick-up. If all goes smoothly, I'll be in Lavender's car by noon. *You know what to say,* I think to myself. My dad walks over to his bed from the bathroom.

"Hey, Dad, I wanna get out of the house for an event today."

"What'd your mom say?" he asks.

"Dunno, she didn't reply to my text," I say, shrugging.

"Well, if you don't hear back from her ..."

I frown. *Why can't I ever just leave home because I want to,* I wonder. My phone buzzes in my hand; I glance downward. Shit. They're five minutes away.

"Okay ... ," I say, backing away casually. "I'll just let you catch some Z's now."

His eyebrow raises slightly, but I ignore it, racing downstairs to grab my jacket when I'm out of view. My hand reaches for the doorknob when my dad suddenly calls my name from the top of the stairwell. My deadname, that is. He says that Mom will be home shortly, therefore I should wait. I eye a car pulling up in the driveway through the kitchen window.

"Can't," I yell back. "Ride is here." With that, I'm out the door.

I slide into the front seat of a red Hyundai Accent.

"Hi, I'm Lavender Sunshine," the brunette-haired driver says to me. "This is my partner, Sal," they add, gesturing to the Black woman wearing a hat and scarf of mixed patterns. "And of course, our friend, Zoë."

Zoë is a white transmasculine person around my age with red bangs swept to the left side of their face. Zoë and Sal share pronouns, and I introduce myself accordingly. As we pull onto the main street, my phone vibrates against my leg.

My mom texted: "Your dad said you left without permission. Where are you and who are you in the car with?" My hand subconsciously reaches to pluck my eyebrow hairs as I consider a response.

"You okay?" Zoë asks. I nod and shut down my phone.

"Don't worry. We'll have a great time," Lavender says with a smile. I deeply hope she's right.

Twenty minutes later, Zoë, Sal, Lavender, and I arrive. In the building's entryway, someone gives us a raffle ticket and wristband. We can also pick up any pronoun pins. I look around. There are dozens of vendors' tables, an energized host making an announcement onstage, and a bar on the far right side. Someone waves at me. Kelsey, my case manager from OUTMemphis, is selling merchandise for the organization, and I happily greet her. My new friends and I agree to meet back up later, so I bound over to the haircut sign-ups.

The barber is pretty booked, so my appointment won't happen for another hour at least. I decide to start the legal name change process with the help of the onsite attorney. She asks me to print my full chosen name. *Easy, Stellan Emir Knowles.* She fills out several blanks, asks me to confirm I'm not changing my name to avoid felony charges, and eventually, her words become drowned out by the growing volume of my thoughts. I'm *actually* doing this? I'm *actually* crowning myself with names that, when combined, mean prince of temperance?

Next, she says I'll have to take this form down to the courthouse, but she mentions OUTMemphis could likely help me overcome the financial burden. That puts the biggest grin on my face. Yes, I *am* doing this.

Close to two p.m., I cross toward the back of the stage to the small room where hair alterations take place. Having taken my hair down in the bathroom, I feel more self-conscious than nervous because of the chaos I witnessed in the mirror. My phone is on now with the picture of my ideal cut prepared. Inside, there are a few people at a table getting nails painted, one person in a chair in front of a blue-haired stylist, and another person in a chair in front of a barber. I ask the barber if I'm next, and he nods. I suddenly think about half-doing it or backing out, beginning to worry I'm making a mistake. My mom always insisted short hair wouldn't look good on me. But I'm sitting down before I know it. Sean, the barber, assures me to go for it if this is what I really want. He can take care of the looking good.

As he raises the buzzing blade up to my head, someone at the nail table says, "You're getting it cut? But your hair is so long and pretty!" I nearly roll my eyes. I want to say, "And that's the *problem* actually," but I can't utter a sound. So I just close my eyes and let Sean work his magic. When I reopen them and see the multitudes of hair clumps falling off my shoulders, I get teary. Now I know how Icarus must've felt as his wings brushed the ether.

I stand up lighter and freer, unburdened by heavy tresses. Sean gave me a really nice fade on the sides with a tall top. Sal snaps a couple pictures of me coming out of the room, and later when I check them, I see I'm giddily flapping my hands and grinning. I'm not hit with feelings of regret at all. That is, until we all pile into the car, and I'm faced with the ride home. Every thought zipping across my mind ends with "?!" A torrent of questions is, of course, a recipe for anxiety. I try to take a few deep breaths, but we're soon pulling into the driveway. The one thing I do know is that *no one* can save me from my parents.

Because I've seen numerous movies showing an adolescent or young adult getting home later than they should, I know how to sneak in stealthily. But my mom steps out from behind her car as soon as I enter the garage. She blocks the door into the house and asks me what I am thinking, coming home looking how I do. She brings up the acting role I am expected to film (where my character has long hair), and I almost start to cry. *Of course*, I know I have obligations, *of course*, I know there's church tomorrow, but what does any of it *matter*? This *whole year*, I've barely felt as alive as I have today. I can't communicate any of this to her, though, so I just take in the reprimand. Well, not exactly.

My brain reminds me of the half-packed backpack I have in my room upstairs, and I start wondering if I'll need to grab it and leave as soon as I'm let in. I tune back in just as someone knocks at the outer garage door. My mom narrows her eyes at whoever she sees in the window. I turn and light up because it's Sal. My friends haven't left me yet, meaning I could be okay after all. I offer to handle introductions as my mom goes to the door. She barely cracks it, but Sal (and the others who've now joined her) seems unfazed. I'm happy that everyone seems cordial, but when Zoë asks if I need anything, my mom butts in with a threat. "I will call the police if you three don't remove yourselves from my property." She promptly slams the door in their faces. I'm stunned. My feet feel made of cement, but I somehow trudge to my room.

I cry myself to sleep that night, dreading the next day and the suffering it will bring. I didn't ask to be alive, to fuck up my life or anybody else's. I'm just trying to exist in a way that feels tolerable since this cold-blooded world will kick me around regardless. But my parents are too blinded by their religion to understand my view.

SUNDAY MORNING: My least favorite day of the week. The mornings invariably go one of two ways: wake up around 6:30 a.m. to be ready for 7:45 a.m. service, attend Sunday school at 9:30 a.m., and leave before 11:00 a.m., OR attend Sunday school at 9:30 a.m., attend 11:00 a.m. "late" service, and leave church close to 2:00 p.m. In my opinion, it's a lose-lose scenario because both involve me stuffing myself into uncomfortable clothes and then sitting uncomfortably to hear a man drone on for ages. So, this particular morning, I agree to attend the later service with my dad and little sister. Similar to yesterday, I'm glad my mom leaves first. My dad can't check on me as I get dressed, so I use that to my advantage. I close my bathroom door and sit on the floor of my annexed closet. If I don't bother to put on church-appropriate clothing, what can he do about it?

Around 8:50 a.m., my dad starts calling for my sis and me to come downstairs for breakfast. I pause then decide to shuffle across to my mom's bathroom because that's what I normally have to do to get jewelry out of her chest or borrow lipstick. I grab my phone and head back. My sister's eyes widen when she sees me, but she doesn't say anything. She's secretly an ally of mine but hates to see me get in trouble. I flop onto my bed, knowing I'm down to the wire. What to say? Despite hating church for years now, I've never outright refused to go—although I was seriously tempted to when my mom explained why I couldn't wear pants. She said it was because her mom, my grandma, "felt the devil on her shoulders" the one time she wore pants to church. Ludicrous, I know.

My dad raps on my cracked door. "You should be ready by now," he says before opening it completely.

"Why aren't you dressed?" he yells.

"I couldn't find anything acceptable to wear."

It's half-true. Most of my dresses are still girl-sized and have gotten embarrassingly short over the years. But what I really mean is, *I don't have any affirming clothes to match my haircut.*

My dad groans. "I'm going to shower and shave. When I'm done, you'd better be ready to walk out the door."

I nod and move toward my dresser. I'm back on my bed when I hear the "beep beep" of the door. Without telling me, he called my mom after he left my room. She's *here.* For the next two hours, they both give me a vehement talking to. I recoil as they assert that *no one will* ever *love me as deeply as they do,* and if I transition to lead a man's life, I will realize that *very* quickly. **Lies!** I think. They may think I don't have common sense, but at the very least, I can see when I'm being manipulated. I glare at them and then send myself to my room. My ears burn from the infuriation building inside me.

SUNDAY EVENING: I hate everything. I've been working on school assignments since early afternoon. My dad's picking up my sister from cheer, and my mom is elsewhere (I don't actually know where). I'm phone-less.

I've just finished submitting a quiz when I get a message on my laptop from Zoë. "Hey, we figure you had a rough night yesterday. Want to go out for some tea, fresh air?"

I've never been more glad to see my texts appearing. "Yes!" I type, immediately finding something to wear.

"Okay, we're on our way."

This starts to feel like the start of yesterday, but I have to make one crucial change. I finish packing my travel bag. I will *not* be coming back. From the office room downstairs, I see my friends pulling into the driveway to the left of the house. (I told them that would be more covert.) I start to run out, but then I see a car pull up behind theirs. It's my mom. Why is she blocking them? Does she recognize their car? I don't know, and Sal texts me not to come out. I feel my chance to escape slipping away. I can't let it! I dart outside in the dark and plant myself in the wooded strip that severs the unrelated properties. My heart is pounding, I'm panting, and some sticks scrape my leg as I creep closer to the situation. It sounds like a heated altercation. Finally, my mom heads to her car and drives over to her driveway. I wait until she's not visible, and then step under the tall streetlight to be seen by Zoë and Sal.

"Stellan!" they exclaim.

I made it.

I'm *free*.

—Stellan Knowles

School Days

I FIRST CAME OUT AS BISEXUAL when I was eleven. For a while, I did not tell many people besides very close friends as I was scared of what the reaction of my peers would be. Later, I was outed to the entirety of my school at twelve. I experienced immense harassment as well as frequent stalking and a few assault attempts. Between the ages of twelve and thirteen, I began exploring my transgender identity. For a period of time, around thirteen, I identified as genderfluid and used he/they pronouns. After a bit, my friends encouraged me to ask one or two of my teachers to use my correct name and pronouns. I did, with a hit and a miss.

The first teacher I asked immediately said no, with his explanation being he wasn't comfortable doing that. The second teacher I asked gave an emphatic yes. She told me she was so proud of me for coming to her and that she was honored I trusted her with this information. With her immediately positive reaction, I thought this conversation had been a win. Unfortunately, after I left school for the day, this same teacher went to the school counselor to ask if it was, in fact, okay for her to use my correct name and pronouns rather than what's on my birth certificate. The counselor then decided the correct way to resolve the situation was to call my parents and ask if it was okay with them.

At the time, my parents were incredibly religious, conservative, and transphobic. They were not okay with this information, and I was ridiculed, dehumanized, and effectively exiled from the family name at thirteen years old. They did not kick me out but kept me under their roof in order to look at me with disgust and confusion and make sure I didn't find the chance to transition. After a couple of weeks of this treatment and my already unsteady mental health, I attempted to take my own life. This did not work, and I ended up in a psychiatric institution.

After my stay, when I was supposed to come back to school, the school guidance counselor asked for a private conversation with me and my mother. When we came in, the counselor asked me to consider switching to another school or to an online school as I had created a "disturbance" within this school. You see, the harassment I had faced had been quite public and led to the suspension of multiple students. I suppose this was *my* "disturbance."

After this interaction, I did, in fact, switch to online school, which was the greatest choice my parents ever allowed me to make. At the new school, I was able to change my name within the school system and start anew. When I introduced myself as Jeb, the other kids only knew me as Jeb. The teacher at this online school was also incredibly accommodating, personable, and comforting. She checked in with me every once in a while to see how I was feeling about transitioning to the new school and my actual transition. She really was a blessing to have after the horrible treatment by my previous school.

Then, when ninth grade rolled around, and high school was imminent, I switched back to public school. I chose one across town so that the number of people who knew me before my transition was as few as possible while still being within my town and district. However, this didn't stop people from finding out. One guy from my math class, we'll call him Jared, was friends with a handful of guys who had gone to my elementary school and a couple from my middle school. I guess Jared talked about me at some point, and they connected the dots that they all knew me, and I was transgender. Jared then added me to a group chat on Instagram with him and his buddies. They proceeded to deadname me, misgender me, and threaten me. Most of them made stupid and offensive jokes or comments, but some were all-out threats. The one that has stuck with me the most, that's still jammed in my head and pops up when I'm trying to sleep, is when one of them explained in full detail how they planned to follow me to a bathroom, corner me, and rape me with a mop. I remember him saying, "I'll rape the transgender out of you." And that's pretty much haunted me since.

Within that same year of school, I was also in an art class. For some reason, this art teacher, who actually is kind of a well-known artist associated with Banksy—his name is Jeffrey Gillette if you want to look him up—really had it out for the trans kids in his classes. In my specific class, there was me and one other trans man; of course, we became really good friends. However, our teacher would purposely misgender us, especially in front of the entire class, so everyone could hear. He also consistently deadnamed my friend since his official school stuff still said his deadname. I even remember him having the balls to misgender me to my dad, who at this point was beginning to come around to the whole transgender thing and did actually try to use my correct pronouns. But I just remember feeling so discouraged because I am an artist. All I wanted to do was create, and I was looking so forward to that class, but that teacher ruined it by holding my personal experience against me.

As someone who has been so public and open about my LGBTQ+ identities, against my will or not, since I was a literal child, I have experienced a lot. I have hundreds of memories of judgment, rude and invasive questions, and looks of disgust, more than my brain will let me remember. The majority of my time in school as a transgender student was negative. As a queer person, in general, it has been negative—I remember someone in seventh grade in my choir class turning around to tell me they'd shock the gay out of me.

But I like to look on the bright side; there have been countless times of camaraderie with fellow queer folks who I've found, and I also have had plenty of my cis-straight peers be genuine and good people to me. Especially after I began testosterone, the amount of hate-filled interactions lessened. I grew into myself, with the help of testosterone and on my own, and people didn't see me as much of a punching bag anymore.

I really hope future students are better to queer folk than my peers were to me.

—Jebediah

How Can I Protect You

Navigating the journey, no GPS
Where is my map, where are we going?
I want to hold your hand and support you

Smother/mother; how do I give you room to grow
When I'm scared to let you go?

As a toddler I protected you from danger with
Foam on corners of tables and baby-proofing supplies
You still fell and hit your head
I comforted you and put Band-Aids on your wounds

How do I protect you from homophobia,
Anti-trans legislation, and don't say gay laws
There is no plastic bubble I can put you in
No armor to wrap around to deflect the hatred and ignorance
No way to shield you from social media and 24-hour news cycles

Advocating, encouraging, building your coping mechanisms
This is my "superpower"
Some days it is not enough ... other days we make it to the
End of the day relatively unscathed

—Carol

Social and Legal
Transitioning

Just Embrace

From summer to fall.

a new face.

Emeralds and jades to garnets and rubies.

A transformation of barren beauty.

But for all we see,

the roots of that tree

still run deep.

Unchanged.

Mind and soul.

For a rose by any other name, is our same

little sweet.

Ten fingers.

Ten toes.

A pulsing heartbeat.
Hear them.
See them.
Say their name.
There is nothing to lose, but so much to gain.
Whether oak or orchid, or in between,
let their leaves unfurl.
Let them be seen.
Let their branches stretch towards sun and sky.
Be in their moment.
Don't ask why.

Just embrace

Excerpt taken from *Just Embrace* by Rula Sinara

WHAT DOES *transitioning* really mean? You will find a lot of different answers to that question, and for each person it means something a little different. For some, transition might mean making some minor changes to the way they present themselves. For others, transition might mean taking hormones and undergoing complicated surgeries. With the extensive range of ways in which a person transitions, it might seem like a complicated term. But in some ways, it is really quite simple.

At its essence, transition is essentially the process of becoming more congruent inside and out.

Most of us accept that to live full and happy lives, we each get to determine our "path." Some people are career-oriented, others are more family-oriented, and some balance the two. There are people who love the big city and those who are happier on a farm. Some like to work with computers, and others with their hands. Some prefer quiet, solitary lives and others are happiest when there is noise and bustle all around. Based on a myriad of individual factors, people choose vastly different pursuits to match their values, their interests, their abilities, and who they believe themselves to be.

Why, then, would we think that transitioning is any less complicated and varied for each individual? It is indeed a process, and that process will take a different route and require a different timeline for each individual. But the goal is essentially the same — to live authentically and feel congruent inside and out.

When we start from that definition, it is hard to object to anyone wanting to transition. Depending on our beliefs, as well as our understanding and experience with gender, we may still have some concerns about the process and timing. We may still have fears and reservations about our family member or friend beginning their transition and what they have planned for themselves. However, when we withhold love and support, we are essentially saying to our loved one, "I do not want you to live authentically and to feel congruent inside and out."

We may not all agree on the age at which transition should begin and how the process should unfold. But can we agree that all people deserve to live authentically, to feel congruent, and to feel that their body is aligned with their sense of self? In order to do so, all persons should have the right to pursue a life free from the distress of gender dysphoria.

Social Transistion

For most people, the first aspect of transition is social. This involves a multitude of variables and is an individualized process.

This type of transition might involve a significant change in hair (cutting it short or letting it grow long), more feminine or more masculine clothing, a change of name, or a change of overall presentation to the outside world. Social transition is the process of beginning to live more authentically as one's true gender. For many youth, this takes a bit of experimentation. It is not uncommon for a teen to try a number of different names, styles, and haircuts before they stumble on the one that feels "most right" for them.

Social transition may also involve confiding in the trusted people in one's life. Many people will tell their family and friends, and may eventually come out at school or work and in their neighborhoods and places of worship. Socially transitioning to live more congruently with how one sees oneself can take a long time. And it may involve some stops and starts as an individual encounters the challenges of transitioning, including rejection from friends or family, teasing or bullying at school, the loss of one's hobby or sport if it were connected to one's sex assigned at birth.

Social transition is not a linear process. And each person proceeds at their own pace. Some prefer the approach of "dip the toe in the water and slowly get in," while others seem to prefer the approach of "rip the Band-Aid off." There is no right or wrong way to socially transition.

Pronouns

For many youth, an early aspect of social transition is to ask others to use the pronouns that feel most right for them. To a teen, the change in pronouns reflects their emerging sense of self, which is simultaneously significant and fraught with emotion. This may mean that a transgender girl (assigned male at birth) requests that others begin using she/her pronouns, or a transgender boy (assigned female at birth) requests that others begin using he/him pronouns. A non-binary person might ask others to use they/them or xe/xem. As a teen continues to evolve in their understanding of themselves, they may change the pronouns they feel fit best. Among those they are close to, the usage of the correct and current pronouns is profoundly important.

To a trans person, usage of their new pronouns conveys understanding, respect, and appreciation for what they have shared about themselves. Hearing the use of their new pronouns affirms that they are being taken seriously, have an ally, and are seen for their true self. Some teens report that the use of correct pronouns is the most crucial factor in feeling accepted by peers or parents.

Many parents will try to use their child's new pronouns but will inevitably make mistakes. Some teens are patient with their parents as they adjust to new pronouns. Others have a tough time speaking up and letting their parents know how important it is to them.

Eventually, as parents and others learn to see a trans teen for who they are authentically, usage of the correct pronouns begins to come more naturally. Before long, it will feel strange to go back to the old pronouns—they simply don't fit anymore.

How did you know which pronoun(s) fit you best?

- I really think about how they make me feel and if they feel like "me." I ask myself if it reflects not only who I am but how I experience my gender, which is something I think about often. If they fit, they're for me!

- I realized that when people used she/her, it felt like they were talking about someone else, and that he/him felt grounded in who I perceive myself to be.

- I still don't think they have been invented yet.

- In Finnish we are lucky to have one pronoun for all: hän.

Names

Another significant aspect of social transition occurs when a child asks to go by a new, more gender-affirming name. In addition to simply needing to adjust to a new name, parents often have difficulty understanding their child's sensitivity to their previous name.

After all, parents spend a lot of time thinking about what to name their unborn baby. They look through lists of names, try different ones on for size, and consider family names and names that hold some level of significance to them. In many ways, this is the first gift that a parent gives their child. It is among their earliest acts of parenting.

But when teens come out as trans or non-binary, they often feel that the name they were given does not represent who they are. Like their parents before them, teens look through lists and consider various names. They often try several in their quest to find one that seems to "fit" them best. And when they settle on a name, it is significant. In some ways, it is the first gift they give *themselves* and one of their earliest acts of breaking away from expectations that caused them distress.

> **To a trans or non-binary teen, having someone begin to use the new name they have chosen for themselves is one of the most significant acts of respect and acceptance.**

Conversely, when the new name is *not* used, especially by a parent, the trans or non-binary teen can feel as if they are not really *seen* for who they truly are. They might say something like, "Stop using my deadname" in order to emphasize that the name they were given is now "dead" to them. It is no longer their name. It doesn't represent who they are. When parents hear the term "deadname," however, it can feel like a rejection and foster a sense of grief.

One way forward is to negotiate the term "given name" instead of "deadname." It acknowledges to the trans or non-binary teen that they did not, in fact, choose that name and may provoke less of an emotional reaction from a parent.

Thoughts from a Therapist ...

For kids who are exploring their sense of gender diversity, trying out new names and pronouns is an important stage. There is no tangible way to know if a name or pronoun fits you other than to have it used. In the teen groups I run, we have an agreement that each member will create a name tag with their pronouns every single week. This emphasizes the permission to experiment. Some kids will use a different name or pronouns each week until they land on what feels best for them.

Appearance

Another important part of social transition is what we call *gender expression*. This might involve a change in clothing, haircut, and other aspects of outward presentation. There are few aspects that suggest gender more definitively than one's hair. We tend to see long hair, especially styled in a "feminine" manner, and we assume the person to be female. Likewise, a short, cropped haircut can easily suggest a person is male. In our culture, men and women tend to wear different clothing. Colors, fabrics, and styles all offer subtle hints as to gender. For this reason, many individuals use these social messages to convey their gender identity. Trans males are likely to cut their hair short and begin to wear more "masculine" clothing. Trans females often grow their hair long, apply makeup, and wear more "feminine" clothing. Many people who are non-binary or agender aim for an androgynous presentation. Some who are gender fluid or gender queer might alternate their presentation between feminine and masculine or even express both simultaneously.

This aspect of social transition often involves time and experimentation to settle on what most accurately conveys one's sense of self. Parents who want to be a part of the process and support their child's social transition can offer to take them shopping or to order clothing online. Free returns are a wonderful option for those experimenting with color, fabric, and style.

Many teens will feel intensely positive and validated when seeing themselves for the first time with a haircut and clothing that matches their inner sense of self. In fact, there is even a name for this positive feeling: gender euphoria. Gender euphoria refers to the positive feeling one has when their gender identity is recognized and appreciated, either as the result of an internal experience (e.g., when one's reflection matches their identity) or as the result of a social experience when one's true gender identity is publicly acknowledged, respected, and celebrated.

Thoughts from a Therapist ...

I have seen numerous kids express with glee how they felt the first time they were able to cut their hair or wear a padded bra. These small changes are incredibly significant in helping a teen begin to see their authentic self reflected back to them in the mirror. Two kids come readily to mind.

Eric had been identifying as a trans male for almost a year. But he had been afraid to come out at his small private school and therefore had not made many visible changes yet. He had begun to wear more gender-neutral clothing but still had a feminine hairstyle. Almost as soon as he came out to his school, he went and got a typically "boyish" haircut. When he showed up for the group that week, he looked lighter, happier, more relaxed, and more comfortable. The smile on his face said it all. He finally looked to the rest of us the way he imagined himself to look all along.

Layla was a teen who had been assigned male at birth. She identified as non-binary but preferred a more feminine appearance. She was quiet in the group and typically shared only about school and hobbies. But one day, she showed up to the group eager to tell the group that she had tried on her first padded bra. She said it felt so good and made her so happy to see herself with a more feminine physique. She had worn it only in the privacy of her bedroom, but the experience was profoundly affirming.

Legal Transition

Often when one has lived socially in their authentic gender for a while, they may decide to legally transition. This involves applying for a legal name change and changing the name and sex marker on the driver's license, passport, and birth certificate. Once legally changed, the name and sex marker must also be changed at school, work, medical offices, etc. This part of the transition can be tedious and cumbersome. In some states, the process is more easily navigated than in others. While the process is a bit of drudgery, the result often leads to a deep sense of affirmation. Many of the youth I work with celebrate when their legal name change arrives in the mail. They are often excited to get their new driver's license and feel that it more accurately reflects who they are.

Thoughts from a Therapist ...

I had been working with Lenny for over a year, and he had been persistently asking his parents to help him make a legal name change. His parents eventually down-loaded the required form and put it on his dresser where it sat untouched for over a month. His mom called me to express concern. Was he "having second thoughts?" she asked. She wasn't sure if she should bring up the topic or not. If he wasn't ready, she didn't want to push him to make the legal change, but she was perplexed because he had been so insistent. I told her that it was not entirely unusual for teens to want their parents to support the legal name change and then not follow through right away. I tried to explain that what Lenny had been really asking for was proof that his parents recognized the permanency of his transition. As soon as his mom left the form for him, he had the proof. Filling out the form was a formality that he would get around to in time, but the insistence had been about assessing his parents' level of acceptance, not the legality of it.

Changes

I'm not like other kids
So let's make some changes
Changes to my hair,
My face,
My style.
I can't live with such dysphoria,
So let's change it all,
In what I believe,
In the shoes I wear.
When asked why,
I will simply reply:
This is who I have always
Been on the inside.

—Ray F.

He/They

I don't know who I Am
I'm a stickler for good grammar, yet
I obtain no pronoun;
however, I possess I/Me, to others I Am You/Your
gender is but semantics
a man is adjectives to compliment the noun
verbs are accessible to all
I maybe, may be, He

I've been here artistically before,
yet look how much I've grown,
and I've closed a door to open a window.
a paper plane that's been flown
when unfolded, then refolded
can sail in the water as a boat
then disintegrates, goes with the flow
I maybe, may be, They

And then

I maybe, no I Am He and They

going to and fro like waves to the shore

I know who I am

to be Him is to simply be Them

and I Am Seamus

Seamus Am Him

I Am Him

Them Am Seamus

Seamus Am Them

I Am Them

Him Am I

Seamus Am Him Am Them Am I Am Him

Gender is only existence explained by semantics.

—Seamus Ruth

The Name

FOR A LONG TIME, we had a jar in our house, and my husband and I had to put a dollar in it every time we misspoke. Not swearing—I would have filled that &*#^$% up in a day. No, it was if we used the wrong pronouns with our teenager.

She had come out to us when she was thirteen, after a long, dark year in which the secret she'd been keeping became too heavy for her to bear any longer. Our boy was actually a girl, she explained, and she wanted us to use she/her pronouns.

Well, of course, we said, eager to help her move on from this place of darkness into her authentic self. But we stumbled. A lot. After the fifth consecutive "he" in an evening, we knew we had to do something to make our daughter believe that our missteps weren't intentional, that we supported her journey. In one of the websites, books, or online discussions I was poring over in my self-directed crash course on gender transitions, I learned about a pronoun jar. If you put some money in each time you use the wrong pronoun—and give your kid the spoils—it injects a little levity and shows your kid that misgendering them doesn't mean you are not on board with their new life. It's just an honest mistake.

Our daughter loved the "She Jar." She loved calling us out on it, watching the dollars add up, and raiding the jar for a trip to the drugstore for her first tentative steps into makeup and nail polish.

And having the "She Jar" was great training for us. Every time we got called out and had to open our wallets, we resolved to do better. We eventually got it, and just as she/her was becoming second nature, our daughter announced she was ready to round another milestone in her journey. She wanted to pick out a new name.

We're behind you 100 percent, we said. But inside ... well, this was a tough one.

Like every parent we know, we invested so much in choosing the perfect name for our child. We pored over baby naming books, we had long lists and short lists, we toyed with origins and meanings, we considered statistics to stay away from names that were too trendy or too popular.

And in our case, we had especially high stakes for picking the perfect, meaningful name. Our kid is adopted from overseas, and, while renaming international adoptees, like everything about adoption, comes with sensitivities about separating a child from their birth culture, we plowed ahead as mindfully as we could. We hoped the name we settled on threaded a needle that wove together our child's birth country and new home.

New family, new country, new start—new name.

So, it was hard not to feel the sting of rejection. The name had been so carefully chosen, and now we're just going to throw it away? Now we're forbidden from ever using it and can only refer to it as the "deadname"?

Turns out, this reaction wasn't unique. I've been in parent support groups, real and virtual, in group therapy, in one-on-one conversations with other parents of trans and gender-expansive kids, read many articles and books, and I heard the same thing over and over—pain and grief at having to give up our children's names.

We parents strive to only let these feelings out in safe spaces, away from our kids so as to never appear unsupportive. The laments are always the same, though: sadness, rejection, maybe even a little measured resistance when we don't immediately love the name our kiddo has chosen.

Every single parent I've talked to has had the same problem with nomenclature. "Why do they have to call it the deadname?" I would hear parent after parent wail. "It's such an awful way to describe it."

A therapist who ran one of my parent groups said, "I've been trying to get teens I counsel to say 'birth name,' but it won't stick. I think they like the finality of the word dead."

In our support groups, we'd talk this through incessantly, those of us who'd been adjusting to a new name comforting the newcomers with their jagged, raw grief. We heard everyone's stories behind birth names—how they were chosen to honor a family member, how they were names parents had been holding onto for years before starting a family, how they were names carefully selected to complement siblings' names.

Change is hard. But sometimes, if you're open to listening, you hear something that reframes the situation so perfectly that the fog you've been grounded in lifts. One night in a support group, a parent sighed, "Well, of course, for any kid, not just kids like ours, the name you give is one you picked before you ever knew them, before you ever knew who they are."

I thought about the story of my own name. My parents left the hospital with newborn me without a name on my birth certificate. They had a few they were toying with but hadn't settled on one. After more than a week, they chose the one they thought suited my emerging personality best.

And just like that, I started thinking that maybe names are more impermanent, less absolute than I had believed. The name I had given my child was anchored deeply in her past. She was ready to choose a name to take her into her future.

In time, the term "deadname" even stopped making me wince. I still don't love the phrase, but I get it. The "deadname" represented a past my daughter was trying to break free from.

The name she chose is traditionally feminine and beautifully lyrical. It's a name with no history in our family in any generation we can trace. It's a name that was never on any of our lists when we were thinking about starting a family. And it's a name that has no ties to her birth country. It's perfect—a name she, herself, chose because what was her coming out but a rebirth?

—B

My Name

THE NAME GIVEN TO ME AT BIRTH is a female name. It's of American origin and supposed to mean "beautiful one." To my parents, it was also the name of my father's best friend, my mother's middle name, and my great-grandmother's name. Meanwhile, my middle name was the feminine iteration of my grandfather's. My name felt unique when I was in school; I was the only one with that name in every class. And at the time, its uniqueness made me feel unique and special.

Now, I don't often disclose my birth name. Professors might have access to it, but I request that they not use it. It's hard to look at. It feels clunky and heavy on my tongue and makes my eyes feel like they might begin to bleed. It sounds like loud and piercing microphone feedback in my eardrums.

It is no longer my name.

For years, I went by a fraction of the name: Ace. The nickname passed as androgynous enough to suffice through my gender identity crises—those hard times in my life when I had no idea who I was in the slightest.

Ace never felt like me though.

Femininity makes me feel disgusting, so the name had to go. I had a lot of ideas: Apollo, Alex, August, and Aziel, just to name a few.

Then, during my sophomore year of high school, I finally realized who I was. I was no longer that little girl. I was Avery Michael Lewis. Same initials as before, just made to better suit my identity.

Avery, to me, means freedom. It means expression, masculinity, androgyny, and truth. It's who I always was underneath the mask. It doesn't bring me discomfort like the last name I had.

And when it is recognized legally, I will finally be me.

—Avery Lewis

Seeing My Reflection

I DIDN'T HAVE ANY HAIR WHEN I WAS BORN. Looking at my 23andMe genetic profile, it seems as though it's the result of a genetic predisposition. Soon enough, brown locks sprouted from my head. They grew and grew, curly and thick and dark. My hair tangled easily, and both Mamaw and Daddy, who looked after me at the time, sometimes brushed it three times a day.

Momma joined the "brushers' union" as the custody agreement allowed but offered a much less gentle hand. She often forced the brush through my hair while tears streamed down my face. Mamaw, after brushing with much gentler strokes, would compliment me on the softness of my hair. Her own was thinner than mine and white, despite her relatively young age.

I remember one day, we were eating vegetable soup in Hot Dog World, and a teenager adorned with rainbow nylon arm sleeves, rubber bracelets, and a black Blood on the Dance Floor T-shirt sat down a few booths away from us with her family. The most striking aspect of her appearance was her rainbow-dyed hair, cut in a choppy style. A zeitgeist of the late 2000s, some might say. Mamaw took one look at the girl's hair, shook her head, and called her crazy. I wonder what she would say about me now.

When I was young, my hair more resembled my aunt's than Momma's. I often got mistaken for my aunt's child. She couldn't have her own kids, so she liked to roll with it. I remember my curls being unruly. Momma says my kindergarten pictures make me look like I have horns. That ended up being a theme in many of my pictures, when the curls decided to point straight up instead of behaving themselves. I never liked having my hair put up. I hated it even. But Momma liked putting bows in my hair and pulling it tight into ponytails. It hurt, but I learned to tolerate the pain.

When I went to live with Momma full time, we cut several inches off my hair. We got my ears pierced too. It felt like a prize, a reward for dealing with Daddy for so long. Looking back, it was more akin to a participant medal than a first-place trophy. My ears were pierced a little crooked, but that's what we got for going to Claire's.

My hair maintained the same approximate length for years, until one fateful trip to Great Clips when I was eleven years old. It was meant to be a routine trim, just removing any split ends and reshaping my layers. The razor burn on the back of my neck was bad enough, but the stylist also left my hair curling up to my ears. I looked like a mushroom. Momma told me short hair would never look good on me; I decided to grow it out immediately.

After that, I let it grow and grow and grow for years. In third grade, before the fateful mushroom cut, a girl at my school told me not brushing it was gross, so I brushed it more. I brushed it dry, which, when you have curly hair, leaves you with a fluffy, frizzy mess. I lived in that mess for five years. My peers, of course, made comments about it. My teachers didn't hold back either. Why does that seem to be human nature?

At thirteen, during the most passionate part of my emo phase, I tried to mold my hair into a deep side part. It didn't work. I was so fixated on making sure everyone knew I had "good" music taste and "good" style, I hoped my Fall Out Boy and My Chemical Romance T-shirts and my requests for their songs to be put in the queue at after-school dances got the point across. Thank God I never got into flat ironing.

At about that time, I met Vinca. We shared a homeroom teacher as well as our accelerated math and English classes. We got close, very close, some might say. Her hair was long and dyed pink, and she wore a pink hoodie to match. She was the first openly queer person I had ever met. I had been indoctrinated by my Southern Baptist upbringing into thinking that being queer was one of the worst things you could be, that it made you evil. And yet, I thought the exact opposite about Vinca. I loved her, but I never, ever wanted to be someone's girlfriend. Only later would I figure out why. Regardless, she made me realize my pansexuality and that I really wanted to dye my hair too. But Momma said she didn't like hair that was "crazy colored." I really had no control over my appearance, which would only be amplified in the coming years.

That summer, at a dance during the summer enrichment program I attended, I donned a black polo shirt and striped, blue tie, then twisted my long mane all into my My Chemical Romance hat. When I walked into my hall's lounge, they thought I was a boy. *That* didn't make me question anything. And I *definitely* did not start expanding my YouTube subscriptions to trans male creators like Miles McKenna and Jamie Raines. Even if I had, that's a *completely* normal, cisgender woman thing to do, *right?*

I knew I wasn't cisgender. I knew I wanted my hair short, but still worried that it would look bad. I asked Momma what she thought—about my hair, not my gender. She agreed it would look bad, my prior mushroom haircut obviously skewing her perception. I asked my first boyfriend what he thought—if I should cut it short or not. He told me that I didn't need short hair to appear more masculine. Part of me thinks his reply was born of his own experience with his parents, who kept going back and forth on allowing him to get a short haircut. I didn't need to live by his restrictions, and yet I did not act. I found myself ducking my head, hiding behind my brown locks when I didn't want to be perceived. Where would I hide if not behind my mask of curls?

Then, in July 2019, my fed-up, fourteen-year-old self decided to have my frizzy curls chopped. After years of turmoil, years of loss of self, I looked in the mirror, and recognition glimmered in my eyes. All the stylist did was buzz the sides and back of my head. She left a little more on top. "Enough to play with." I had come out to myself as a trans man over a year earlier. I had told my friends a matter of months earlier. Prior to that, I had searched for an online community, for resources and advice. I had seen trans masculine people online say that buzzed styles with more length on top were good means of masculinizing your face. My mom immediately thought I was a lesbian. She was a little bit off on that assumption and found out the truth when I was outed less than a month later.

I had found myself but had yet to dye my hair. I wanted color in it so badly. Maybe red? Maybe blue? Maybe red with black sides? When I asked my boyfriend how he thought I'd look, he told me he thought dyeing my hair would make me ugly. I remember wondering why my attractiveness would be conditional if he really loved me. I still don't have an answer.

Quarantine hit and we were responsibly staying in. Momma offered to let me dye my hair—perhaps because we wouldn't be going out in public, where she might get embarrassed by my appearance. Thanks to my boyfriend's influence, I turned down Momma's offer. I didn't want him to find me ugly. After our inevitable separation, I asked Momma again if I could take up her offer, but her attitude had already changed again, for reasons she would never even allude to. Because, of course, I could only be myself if I was hiding behind the screen on a school Zoom call.

Eventually, I went away to boarding school. Dyeing my hair was not at the forefront of my mind. That is, until the twins, fellow trans people living at the far end of my hall, had extra dye left over from their own hair-coloring adventures. They offered their excess to anyone who wanted it. It was a spur-of-the-moment decision. Those impulses at two a.m. have a way of winning me over, but I didn't regret this one. I still don't, besides the fact that the dye never really washed out. Now I know that the brand "Splat" is more similar to printer ink than anything else.

My next experiment was a blue undercut, with my natural brown on top. Then blue all over. Later, I went blond all over. Then, my hair got a bit too long, and it was time for a dorm room haircut. So, the blond disappeared, buzzed right off the sides and back of my head. We, my pseudo-stylist roommate and I, decided to leave some blond on top. As hair does, the blond kept growing out. I got tired of the natural hair peeking from beneath it, so I dyed all my hair red. Then came an odd iridescent brown, born from trying to neutralize the red with green dye. Color theory was too hard, so I gave up and dyed my whole head black. With no clear next color, I let the black fade and grow out. Currently, my hair is its natural brown shade with slightly lighter tips.

Who knew having control of your own hair could be so empowering? The people I truly love, and who truly love me, don't care about my hair. Ironically, Momma does, but she's changed her tune once more. It turns out she misses the faded blue. I never got to find out what Mamaw thought, and I guess I never will unless she figures out how to talk from six feet under. The first thing Nana, my last living grandmother, told me last Thanksgiving was that she liked the blond better.

She passed after I told her of my manhood but before I could break this truth to her: my appearance—hairstyle and color, way of dress, way of carrying myself—is not for anyone but me. My appearance, my body, my rules, my decisions, forevermore.

—Donnie Wilkie

Medical
Transitioning

Just Embrace

Let their souls stir and sing,
like birds in spring.
None lesser.
None better.
Each transformation captivating,
like redbud flowers blossoming
straight from wood.
Forget the expected and the 'should.'
Children are the future.
Change is good.

And life is a fundamental right.

No one needs to hide in the bitter darkness of night.

No one forced to beg to JUST BE.

To exist rightfully ... fully.

To explore and discover who they're meant to be.

The glorious rainbow

and all between.

Let them be loved.

Let them be seen.

Excerpt taken from *Just Embrace* by Rula Sinara

NOT ALL GENDER-DIVERSE PEOPLE FEEL the need to medically transition. Some are satisfied with their social or legal transition, or both, and do not feel they need to make changes to their body to affirm who they are. However, for others, physical changes are crucial, and medical transition is the only way to fully relieve their gender dysphoria.

The process of medical transition is as varied and as nuanced as the process of social transition, but even more complicated and costly. For each person, the path will be different and options vary according to state laws. For detailed information, talk to a medical provider in your state about the variety of options available for medical transition. In the meantime, we will look at three primary components of medical transition that are most commonly spoken about: hormone blockers, hormone therapy, and surgical options.

Hormone Blockers

For younger individuals, who have either just started puberty or who have entered puberty recently, hormone suppression therapy (more commonly referred to as "hormone blockers") can provide some important relief from the distress of developing further as a man or a woman. Hormone blockers are not new, nor are they reserved for transgender kids. They have been used for many years to pause the development of secondary sex characteristics for kids who have a precocious puberty, meaning they enter puberty at an early age that is not socially appropriate.

Hormone blockers operate essentially as a "pause" button. They specifically target the development of secondary sex characteristics. Current studies indicate that hormone blockers do not affect other aspects of growth and development.

We all need hormones, so no one can exist on hormone blockers indefinitely. There are two ways to add hormones back into the body. The first is to simply stop using hormone blockers and allow natal puberty to resume. The second is to introduce cross-sex hormones and allow the person to enter puberty that is consistent with their gender identity. Sometimes hormone blockers are used in conjunction with hormone therapy to suppress natal puberty while supporting the desired puberty.

For many kids and their parents, the use of hormone blockers offers the gift of relief and time. Relief for the young teen who dreads physical bodily changes that are foreign to their sense of self, and time for parents to research, learn, get support, talk to therapists and medical providers, and begin to make decisions in the best interest of their family.

Hormone blockers are also essentially reversible. At a certain point, they are discontinued. However, puberty is *not* reversible. The changes that one experiences during puberty cannot be reversed. Voice changes for natal males, breast development for natal females ... these will remain with a person once they have occurred. This means that a trans female will have to contend with a deepened voice, and a trans male will likely want breast removal surgery later in life. Hormone blockers provide a way to avoid these changes until decisions can be made.

teen talk

What was your experience with hormone blockers?

- It's been really great! It's been gentle and better than birth control. It's given me the freedom to not have to suffer and deal with horrid dysphoria and allows me to be myself and think about anything other than my body for a little bit.

- They were so helpful in giving me more time to think about what I wanted for myself.

- I have never taken hormone blockers, but I have taken birth control, because I'm not brave enough for HT.

- I started in 7th grade, and at that point, I was taking something just to stop my period. It helped me feel so much better about my body.

- I'm attempting to get on them, but they were just banned in my state.

- I was on them for a year, starting at age twelve, and they had an enormous impact on my mental health, greatly reducing gender dysphoria.

Hormone Therapy (HT)

As already mentioned, we all need hormones. At some point, we must either allow the natal puberty to resume or medically orchestrate a puberty that is more consistent with a person's gender identity. In this case, many trans teens and young adults pursue hormone therapy.

For those who are assigned male and whose gender identity is female, estrogen and progesterone might be prescribed. These hormones activate a process that will move the teen into a puberty typical of a natal female.

For those assigned female at birth and whose gender identity is male, testosterone would be prescribed. This can be taken in a few different forms and initiates a typical male puberty.

As is true for cisgender teens, hormone therapy initiates puberty, which brings an array of changes, some desired and some not. It is important that any teen undergoing hormone therapy fully understand the changes that will occur and accept the reality that changes cannot be "cherry-picked." Along with the changes they are seeking, teens must accept the ones they might prefer not to encounter.

For minors, parental permission is required to obtain any medical treatment, including hormone therapy. In addition, current laws and medical standards require that a qualified mental health provider thoroughly assess a minor and their history of gender incongruence to determine that hormone blockers are recommended or that hormone therapy is medically necessary to relieve diagnosed gender dysphoria. Only with appropriate documentation of this gender evaluation, and upon the recommendation of the mental health provider, is the minor even seen by a medical provider who would consider prescribing any treatment that would affect gender development. This is a rather lengthy and involved process that can take between six months and several years, depending on the availability of the qualified mental health professional or the medical provider. It seems critics who express that minors are given medical treatment in an impulsive, hasty, or irresponsible fashion do not understand the arduous process minors and their parents endure before receiving any gender-affirming medical care.

The decision to seek gender-affirming medical care is often an emotional and complicated one for both minors and their parents. Even when minors are steadfast and determined, and a mental health provider has supported the decision, some parents feel more comfortable requiring their teen to wait until they are eighteen, thereby relieving themselves of the burden of making such a weighty decision for their teen. Sometimes, these parents realize later that they traded one burden for another and carry the weight of having required their teen to continue to develop in ways that can never be reversed (voice drop, facial hair) or that will need to be surgically altered later (breast development).

Current research indicates that mental health outcomes are better for those trans youth who transition earlier, and sometimes parents look back and wonder if they could have spared their teen some of the anguish of living with gender incongruence if they had allowed the medical transition to begin earlier. This is not to suggest that parents are *wrong* to require their teen to wait until the age of majority to begin medical transition. It is simply important to note that whether they grant their permission for a minor to medically transition or require that they wait, parents of trans youth face a difficult decision and carry a burden in either case. Parents facing this heavy decision deserve validation, guidance, and support.

teen talk

What was your experience like with hormone therapy?

- Amazing so far. I do my shots myself and though I forget every once in a while, it is something I have never regretted and 100 percent never will.

- I have not started them. It is difficult to process the information on how to start them.

- I started middle of 8th grade, and my parents have said there was a noticeable change in my confidence and overall energy levels. I feel amazing, and I love all the changes that I'm seeing.

- I admit I've had it a lot easier than others, but it's a struggle to obtain hormones. Changes are slow and start out a little shitty, but the pros seriously outweigh the cons.

- I am so so grateful for my testosterone shots! It was a struggle to get started and continues to be a struggle to find continued care, even in Southern California, but HT has saved my life.

- It was life-changing, but in the best way possible. A variety of things started changing, and at times, it was hard to keep up with it, but now that I'm three years on T, it's way more consistent.

- *I had to wait until I was eighteen to start, and I pay for them with my own income and received them through tele-health—I have been taking testosterone for four months now. My parents aren't aware, only a few people know. I am seeing changes I like already.*

- *Taking testosterone and starting that journey not only saved my life but greatly improved it. Seeking out gender-affirming care for me was a momentous act of self-love. It was me saying to myself that I was worth living for.*

- *I haven't been able to start them. Endocrinologists are booked out months on months, and it became actively illegal for a medical professional to prescribe me HT. Even before that, my endocrinologist didn't trust that I knew I wanted HT since I am non-binary. He said explicitly that if I were a binary trans man, I would've been able to get the medical care I need. My mother has also been very apprehensive.*

Gender-Affirming Surgery

It is important to note that gender-affirming surgery is generally reserved for adults, and as previously stated, not all transgender or non-binary individuals seek surgery as part of their transition. Some feel surgery is not necessary for them to feel content, whole, and happy. Others cannot afford the costs associated with the lengthy and rigorous process of obtaining gender-affirming surgery. Currently, in the US, it typically requires the assessment and documented recommendation of two mental health providers to even get a surgical consultation. The assessment and documentation process costs time and money. The consultation costs time and money. And while more and more insurance companies are covering the financial costs of gender-affirming surgical procedures, where deemed medically necessary, there is time off from work and the costs of postoperative care associated with each procedure that must be considered.

The willingness to persevere despite the challenges of time, energy, and finances only underscores the critical role that surgical intervention plays for those who require it to relieve their gender dysphoria and live authentically.

Most surgeries are divided into one of two broad categories, briefly described below:

Top surgery

For trans males, this means the removal of breasts and the reconstruction of the chest. For trans females, this means breast enhancement. These surgeries are far from cosmetic. They are medically necessary, gender-affirming treatment options to remedy what is often debilitating gender dysphoria. In some states, top surgery is available for older teens, with parental permission and the recommendation of a qualified mental health provider. For many trans and non-binary teens, top surgery is an extremely important aspect of their transition and allows them to feel more comfortable moving through society and being accurately perceived.

Thoughts from a Therapist ...

As I talked to Jim about his upcoming top surgery (double mastectomy with chest reconstruction), I noted the smile on his face and excitement in his voice. Jim had been living as a trans male for over four years and had wanted top surgery for a while. As he explained it, he wanted his "top half to look the way it should, even if the lower half didn't."

I thought back on the many clients who had chosen to have top surgery. In every case, there was a sense of excitement. They looked forward to the surgery! They knew, full well, that there would be a period of several weeks of discomfort, limited movement, and post-operative care. None of that seemed to diminish the joy of being on the cusp of this surgery. I imagine that gender-affirming surgeries are among the very few that people actually look forward to ... after all, few surgeries offer a sense of increased congruence and personal satisfaction the way top surgery does.

Bottom surgery

There are a variety of surgical options available for adults whose genitalia cause significant dysphoria. A decade ago, bottom surgery was less common. The techniques had not been perfected, and there were often complications. While complications are possible with any surgery, the procedures for gender-affirming surgery have become more sophisticated over the past few years, providing an appealing option to many. However, it is still a multi-step, complicated procedure that requires months of recovery. The fact that some people choose to undergo such a surgery is a testament in itself to the strong need to live authentically.

FOR BOTH TOP AND BOTTOM SURGERY, there are numerous variations and options available, and surgical approaches vary among surgeons. A thorough understanding of them is not needed to appreciate the stories that follow. If you, or your family member, are considering surgical intervention, it's important to explore all your options and consult with one or more providers to ensure that you are fully informed and choosing the best path forward. And, again, not all trans persons feel that surgery is needed in order for them to live authentically.

teen talk

What was your experience like with top surgery:

- *Top surgery was the most radical act of self-love and self-care I have ever engaged in. It has completely transformed my relationship with my body and with life.*

- *I am currently saving money for top surgery.*

- *Overall positive. Easy recovery. Worst part was the drains.*

- *It was certainly something, but I am so much more comfortable with myself now.*

- I had a wonderful outcome, and I finally feel like I look good.

- The feeling of being able to be shirtless is life-changing.

- It has been about a year since I began the process of reaching out, and about a year and a half since I began researching. My surgery is in a month. It has been an incredible emotional roller coaster full of dysphoria and euphoria and doubt.

- So far, we're choosing surgeons, it's a little tricky since we have to consider insurance and age. I'm a minor, but hopefully, I will be able to have my surgery during winter break of this upcoming school year.

- I love my chest. I feel free.

- I haven't gotten it, but I really want to. My mom won't let me though because of the scars that I would get from it, but I don't care about the scars.

Assessing Readiness

Most parents want to know how to gauge whether their teen is ready to start medical transition. There is no one answer that fits all gender-diverse teens.

One popular "litmus" test is to assess the degree to which a youth is *consistent, persistent, and insistent* in their gender identity. However, for a variety of reasons, this may or may not apply to all teens. A teen may not be consistent (across all areas of their life) in their gender identity if it means forfeiting a favorite sport or leaving a gendered team of close friends. A teen might not be persistent (out as transgender for a significant period of time) if they live in circumstances where they have not been exposed to gender diversity and have suddenly and conclusively realized that this is an explanation for years of sensing an incongruence within. And some teens are not insistent (strongly asserting one's conviction) in any area of their life, so to require it in such a vulnerable area is unfair. The consistent, persistent, and insistent litmus test can be used as a general guide but should never be used as "criteria" for medical transition.

Neither should social confidence, school performance, or mental health be used as criteria for medical transition. Asking a teen with gender dysphoria to be more social, do better in school, or have better mental health *before* allowing medical transition is like telling a person to stop bleeding before you give them a bandage. The bandage stops the bleeding in the same way that medical transition helps a teen feel more comfortable socially, be more focused on school, and overcome depression and anxiety.

So, how do we know when a teen is ready to begin medical transition? We listen to them. We get to know them and their gender journey. We assess their level of certainty (using the litmus test as a general guide, but not hard and fast criteria). We ask them questions and assess their current level of support and where additional resources may be needed for this stage of transition. And we believe them when they say that they know who they are and how they can best embody their authentic self.

We should also keep in mind that the changes brought about by medical transition are gradual and take time. As a person moves through their medical transition, adjustments can be made in collaboration with their medical provider.

parent perspective

What are your hopes and fears for your child pursuing medical transition?

Common Fears

- *Permanent change that can't be undone.*

- *That medical transition will not solve everything.*

- *Abuse and violence because he is different.*

- *Chronic health issues.*

- *I worry about their desires to reproduce later.*

- *Side effects of various things.*

- *The long-term effects aren't clear, and I don't want my kiddo regretting any of his choices.*

- *That there are underlying mental health issues that also need to be addressed,*

- *The medical risk of any medication or procedure.*

- *The likelihood for violence from haters.*

- *Expensive, painful.*

- *I fear they will later regret having altered their biology.*

Hopes

- *That it will save her life.*

- *I want them to feel comfortable in their body.*

- *That he becomes more comfortable and self-confident enough to do all the wonderful things that life has in store for him.*

- *Just to be herself.*

- *Happiness as she walks through this world.*

- *To find confidence and comfort in his skin, so he can be his true self and find joy.*

- *That these treatments, surgical, nonsurgical, therapeutic support, and a strong network within the LGTBQ community, will help her feel complete from the inside and out.*

- *That she will learn to love the person she was meant and born to be.*

- *I want them to feel comfortable in and even proud of their body.*

- *I want them to look in the mirror and recognize themselves*

Taking T

TAKING TESTOSTERONE AS A TRANS MAN has been absolutely life-changing for me, and I can confidently say it's one of the best decisions I've ever made. From the very beginning, I felt a sense of alignment between my body and my identity that I had never experienced before.

Physically, the changes have been incredible. Watching my body transform has been a source of immense joy and validation. My voice has deepened, and I finally recognize the reflection in the mirror as the true me. The growth of facial hair and changes in body composition have given me a newfound sense of confidence.

But it's not just about the physical changes; it's also about how it's transformed my mental and emotional well-being. The feeling of being more in tune with my gender identity has boosted my self-esteem and self-assurance. I walk through life with a newfound sense of confidence and authenticity.

Taking testosterone has allowed me to live as my authentic self, unburdened by the dysphoria that plagued me before. I'm more comfortable in my own skin than ever before, and it's made every aspect of my life more fulfilling. It's not just about looking different; it's about feeling different, in the best possible way.

I've learned so much about resilience and self-discovery on this journey, and I wouldn't trade it for anything. The decision to take testosterone has been a profound and empowering experience, and I'm grateful for the newfound confidence and happiness it has brought into my life.

—Anonymous

Joy

Joy is the years that have passed between
    my long hair hitting the floor
and facial hairs in the bathroom sink.
It's the years that have passed between the croaky, flat voice
and the first gruff, modulated "hello."
Joy is the years that passed between
    accepting I'll never be a father
to hearing the soft voice that calls me "Dad."
It is the years between binders and bare skin,
between the someday soons and my first injection,
between the "just make it through one more day,"
to the "I can't wait until tomorrow."
Joy is every moment leading up to this day,
the day when I can share my joy with the young
    man behind my steady, tired eyes
when I look in the mirror and tell him:

"You are more than enough,

and you always have been.

Every fiber of your being is destined to be

the man you were always told you couldn't be.

Every year,

every month,

every moment,

has led up to this day.

One day, you will find joy in every version of

     yourself that carried you here to me."

—Alec Williams

Angel Wings

Angel wings
Ripped from my back
Because I had said:
"I know who I am!"
I shall not ascend
With torn up spine
The papers have spoken:
"Your death is all mine."
But keep this in mind,
Those who have stolen—
My life after death
Will keep others hoping
For I've bandaged your wounds
And flattened my chest
I've cut all my hair
And made it a mess
So in every moment
That you've wished and
you've prayed
For me to shrink,
And waste away
Know that your words,

Are things I outlast
Know I lived bigger
In this life, than past
I've lived a grand life
Full of love and of meaning
So when I do pass
And you hear angels weeping
Pull them close
And let them know;
"You cannot kill what does not die."
For from my grave
You'll hear me cry:
I'm alive, I'm alive, I'm alive

—Elena Chamorro

Old Days

An intereview with a trans musician

TÖM HAS BEEN WRITING SONGS even before he reached adulthood, before he came out as non-binary, and before he started testosterone. One day, he discovered an old recording of one such song and decided to fully produce and release the recording as a way of reclaiming his true voice over the high-pitched voice on the track that never fit him in the first place.

Since it is impossible to include the song here, what follows is an excerpt from an interview with TÖM about his gender journey and the evolution of the song.

How did music become such a big part of your life?
My dad plays guitar and has always been involved in country music. He did a lot of live performances in my hometown. When I was thirteen or fourteen, he handed me a mandolin. My sister had already been learning guitar, so he sat us around the kitchen table and basically had us play bluegrass music together. My sister always wanted to be the lead singer, so I started learning how to harmonize. Singing immediately made me appreciate vocals, especially layered vocals. I began noticing things, with vocals in particular, that other people might not notice without that experience.

Eventually I went from mandolin, which is more like a blue-grass instrument, to ukulele. That's when I began singing by myself, doing my own take on vocals. At first, I started learning jazzy, old-timey songs because I liked the way female singers sang back then, like Patsy Cline. These songs felt more genderless and gave me a detachment from how female vocals are supposed to sound with today's expectations of modern femininity.

Once I started having more of an understanding of music theory—how to write a song, rather than throwing it randomly together—I started writing my own songs and singing.

How old were you when you first realized you might be gender diverse? How soon after did you come out?
My oldest memory is from the fifth grade when they told all the girls "what a period is gonna be" and explained feminine hygiene products. I remember coming home that day a mess, crying. I remember it vividly because I was filled with such dread and anxiety but didn't have the vocabulary or language to understand it. I tried to explain how I was feeling to my parents, but they told me that "everyone has anxiety about this," and "it's not that bad." From a cis perspective, this is probably true, but what I felt did not feel normal, and I had no way of verbalizing that.

I came out as bisexual when I was fifteen. It didn't go well with my parents, so I think that's partly why it took me so much longer to figure out the rest. My mom was not necessarily unsupportive, but my dad, who is not supportive of me whatsoever, said things like, "You're too young to understand; you can't possibly have any sort of identity yet because you're only fifteen."

I didn't even know what non-binary was until I was eighteen, when I graduated and moved to Georgia, about twenty minutes outside of Atlanta. I started going to Atlanta a lot and meeting all these different people, queer people, and that's when I started learning about all the different identities. It was shortly after that I came out as non-binary and started transitioning to trans masc.

How did your relationship with your voice change after you came out?

When I started doing makeup and stuff to be more affirming to my gender, I was not particularly dysphoric about my face or body type. I'm still not particularly dysphoric about them. And it's not that I wanted to center my transition around "passing" or making that the mark for success, but my voice was the one thing that people were like, "Oh, that's a trans guy." I felt like as soon as I opened my mouth, especially in my conservative hometown, people started seeing me as a tomboy instead of as a man. This was very, very hard for me. I felt like I had the look I wanted, but that almost made my female voice more obvious to me.

When did you start hormone therapy?

At first, I was just doing makeup to look more masculine, like I'd put on what looks like five o'clock shadow. Then I decided to start testosterone right before my twenty-first birthday, which was a huge decision for me. I made that goal to start testosterone before I turned twenty-one, because I knew I was going to start going to bars and entering these adult spaces, and I absolutely dreaded the idea of being introduced by my deadname or having to reintroduce myself to all those people later.

Were you concerned that HT might affect your singing voice?

I knew that taking testosterone would either really change or not really change my voice. If it didn't really change my voice that much, at least I'd know in my heart that I had pursued it for myself.

That being said, it was hard because people like my dad and others used my voice to blanket their transphobia. The main thing that he and others would point out was, "Oh, you have such a beautiful voice, you're going to ruin it by taking T."

Ruin is such a subjective word, and they're not entitled to my voice. Any artwork I ever create with my voice is something I consensually put out as a gift. No one is entitled to my voice, no matter what I sound like.

Did HT hurt your singing voice?
Within the first year of starting testosterone, I became frustrated. It was like puberty—my voice started changing and cracking without quite settling yet. I felt like I couldn't sing as well. I knew it would eventually settle, and I would be able to sing again in the way I've always wanted, like now. I can sing really low. Even just talking is affirming to me.

In that time of waiting, it did feel like I sort of limited myself, but that's when I began to get into folk punk music where they don't really sing melodically. They more shout over the music. I felt like I could do that really well, so I started leaning into that more edgy sound, and that really helped.

There was no way I was going to go without singing, even if I didn't really have a singing voice. There are so many famous and successful singers who are known for having "non-conventional" or straight-up bad voices, and their music is still just so raw and cuts to the core because of that specifically.

What made you go back to that old song with your old voice?
It was years later that I found the original sound files on an old computer, and I thought, "Like wow, this is actually a good song." I had a whole other identity by then. Most of the people in my

life didn't even know this younger version of me. It was also the perfect opportunity because it was during COVID when everyone was in quarantine. I made so much music then.

I spent a good amount of time producing the song that time around because I wanted it to have the sound that it has, with layered instrumentals. It was a vulnerable piece for me, especially with the vocals recorded before I got on testosterone. With other music up until that point, I mixed the vocals, so my voice sounded lower. The result didn't really sound like me, but I liked how it sounded, and it was a really cool way to explore how I wanted to sound. With this song, I decided not to down-pitch the vocals.

I sent it to one of my close friends, who is trans femme, and asked them what they thought of it. They said, "If you don't release this, I'm going to be personally offended because it is so good." I remember that conversation really well because I'm so grateful for that person.

What did it mean to you to release the song?
I think a lot of what empowered me to end up releasing the song was having been surrounded by all those people who told me, "Oh, you're going to ruin your voice," or "This voice is the staple of your identity."

I never wanted to center myself around my voice. There were and are so many more important things to me than being a good singer, like being a happy person. So, when I decided to produce the song, when I heard the final weight of it, I realized that it was okay that I sounded like that back then, and it's okay that I have this whole other part of my identity now. The people who understand that are the people who will actually listen to my music and hear what I'm trying to say, no matter how I sound.

In releasing the song, I wanted people to know that the art you put out into the world doesn't have to define you or keep you in one spot. That's the vision I had when I was making it.

Any last words?
Just that if it wasn't for my relationship with music, it would have been a lot harder for me to come to the conclusions I did about my identity, especially my goals, because the dysphoria was always there. When you have a creative outlet to let yourself go anywhere, it really helps ground you.

I also want people to know that art exists to get into the nitty gritty parts of yourself, the insecurities that you may be uncomfortable with, so that you can find the beauty in those parts and heal.

—TÖM

Vessel

I understand
My body is
A blank canvas
Waiting
To be painted
Nothing more
A vessel
For my soul
But an ill-fitting one at that
It is too tight and too loose
Too heavy and too light
All at the same time
Like a too-small winter coat
Soaked in water
So I do what I can to make it fit
Tattoos
Piercings
Surgeries
Painted nails
Long hair
3 hours in the gym
5 days a week

And 50 mg of

Testosterone every day

Make it feel a little more

Like home

A little less like looking at

A stranger

In the mirror

But I cannot help

But envy

Those born in one

That fits a little better

—Kai

Other Topics

Just Embrace

Shrinking
behind a silent wall.
Shutting out one and all.
The calm before the storm.
The quiet before the fall.
The fear.
The dread
of bloodshed.
Of listlessness in bed.
Hanging on by a thread.
To cradle and rock in agony,
begging
come to me.

But a broken bough doesn't always fall.
Bend.
Catch it,
cradle and all.
For that which bends will not break.
That is what's at stake.

What kind of world has apathy toward empathy?
Why can't we learn from history?
It's an unconscionable evil to steal peace of mind.
Security and serenity are for all living kind.

Just embrace

Excerpt taken from *Just Embrace* by Rula Sinara

THERE ARE A FEW OTHER TOPICS that deserve mention because they play a prominent role in the life of many gender diverse people. Mental health issues and autism are rather common among transgender people and religion is often a particularly complicated topic for trans people and their families.

Mental Health

There is no doubt that trans youth suffer more mental health issues than their cisgender peers. They are prone to anxiety, depression, eating disorders, drug use, and school avoidance. The suicide rate among trans youth is the highest of any demographic.

> **However, it is important to note that mental health challenges are *not* because they are trans or gender non-conforming. These mental health challenges stem from being trans or gender non-conforming *in a culture* that does not support them.**

Most, if not all, trans and non-binary teens will experience some degree of social anxiety. Every time they step out into the world, they risk the discomfort and awkwardness of being misgendered. Social interactions carry assumptions based on one's sex, and these situations may be extremely counterintuitive to a trans youth. Their parents try, without success, to get them to "go out with friends" or "invite some people over" or "get involved at school" or join a community activity. But their social anxiety might make this nearly impossible.

The mental health challenges experienced by our trans youth are a result of a society that feels hostile to them. Yet, when trans youth come out, and their parents, coaches, teachers, and others support them in their transition, the mental health challenges abate. Kids who have been diagnosed with social anxiety since childhood often become comfortable and outgoing once they socially transition and can be seen in the world for who they really are. So often, depression subsides, kids return to school, eating disorders resolve, and drug use stops. The realities of minority stress will never go away, but when trans youth are allowed to be true to themselves, and when this is celebrated by those around them, they do not suffer mental health challenges any more than the average population.

The mental health challenges experienced by trans youth are the responsibility of us all. We are a part of the society that feels hostile to them. It is incumbent upon every one of us to learn more, to better understand, to find ways to challenge the status quo, and to support trans youth and their parents in order to address the mental health crisis and the high suicide rate among this group of vulnerable kids.

Thoughts from a Therapist ...

Davey had been diagnosed with social anxiety when he was quite young, long before he told his parents that he was a boy and wanted to be called Davey. He had struggled with some depression, too, but anxiety limited his world. When I first started working with Davey, his parents were still in denial that he was trans male but open to learning and committed to helping Davey in any way they could. Over the course of the next year, Davey remained rather reclusive. He attended school in the one large "hoodie" sweatshirt that he felt most comfortable in. He came home after school and stayed in his room. He had some online friends and was occasionally invited by kids in his neighborhood to come "hang out" but rarely went.

About a year into our work together, his parents allowed Davey to take testosterone as hormone therapy. Davey's voice lowered, and he began to have a more male physique. The summer after he started on testosterone, Davey agreed to go to a nearby day camp for kids interested in writing. He showed up as Davey, in his male clothes and with his lower male voice. No one there knew him as anything other than Davey. He was completely accepted and embraced as a boy. We spent several therapy sessions talking about the profound experience this was for him. For the first time in his life, he didn't feel self-conscious about what everyone else was thinking or saying about him. For the first time in his life, he felt that he could just BE himself.

Davey is one of many youth I have worked with whose mental health challenges were directly rooted in their gender dysphoria. For many trans teens, transitioning allows them to be accurately perceived, and as they participate in society as their authentic self, their mental health struggles subside.

If you are a teen: You are not alone. There are other kids like you, and they are experiencing similar challenges. There is also help out there. You don't need to try to manage all these uncomfortable feelings and situations alone. Let your parents know that you want to see a therapist well-trained in gender diversity. Seek out an online community; join an alliance club at school. Things will get better.

If you are a parent: You are not alone either. There are other parents in distress as their child struggles. It is important to take these mental health struggles seriously. Do not dismiss them as "typical teenage troubles." If your child is showing signs of significant distress, find a therapist to help them navigate these challenging times. And find a therapist or support group for *yourself* too. There is likely a long process ahead, and you will find that not everyone understands what is happening in your family. You deserve the support from others who do.

If you are a therapist: Understand that some of the mental health challenges you are seeing in your client might have an underlying theme of gender incongruence. In this case, the typical approach to anxiety, depression, school avoidance, drug use, or eating disorders may not be wholly effective or even appropriate. If you are not already well-trained in gender diversity, seek training or consultation in order to best support your teen client and their family.

Autism

There is a significant amount of overlap between the autistic and transgender communities. Both communities have been misunderstood, marginalized, and maligned. There is a long history of dehumanizing language and mistreatment of both gender-diverse and autistic individuals. In the past, autism has been seen as a disorder based on externally recognized behaviors and something to be cured. In truth, neither gender diversity nor autism is a disorder. Both are naturally occurring.

Autism is a genetically based difference in one's neurology.[3] Autistic nervous systems take in more information than average and process it through a nervous system that perceives sensory experiences to be stronger than expected and generally unpredictable. Lights can be brighter, sounds can be louder, and a light touch can cause pain. The neuro-typical world is often experienced as overwhelming, and the autistic person is blamed for their reaction instead of the environment being recognized as inhospitable. Autistic people often have high intelligence and excellent pattern recognition. They love to dive deep into subjects that interest them and are incredibly creative. They have much to contribute to our society.

When one regularly interacts with either the gender-diverse community or the autistic community, the overlap between the two becomes clear. No one is quite sure why this is, but the fact is undisputed. Some wonder if there may be a genetic tie. Others suggest that an autistic person's tendency to be unconstrained by cultural rules and norms leads naturally to an increased exploration of self, including gender and sexuality. Many autistic people, even if they identify as cisgender, don't connect with the social constructs of gender as they exist within our culture.

Gender-diverse people who are autistic are at a disadvantage when it comes to receiving gender-affirming care. Autism is sorely misunderstood, resulting in the false assumption that autistic people lack the ability to know themselves or use good judgment in decision-making. This false narrative is often used against them. As of this writing, multiple states in the US are attempting to codify into law a denial of gender-affirming care for autistic people. A new perspective on autism and respect for the autonomy of autistic people is desperately needed.

---

3   Nick Walker, *Neuroqueer Heresies: Notes on the Neurodiversity Paradigm, Autistic Empowerment, and Postnormal Possibilities*, (Autonomous Press, 2021).

There is exciting work being done in the area of overlap between neurodiversity and gender diversity. Neuroqueer theory, developed by Dr. Nick Walker, is helping us find language and power in rejecting both neuronormative and heteronormative expectations of society. Those who are autistic and trans exist in this space naturally, and the more support they have in being their true selves, the greater their ability to thrive. Both autistic and gender-diverse people have a measure of integrity, intelligence, and creativity that our society desperately needs. Marginalizing these two populations hurts us all.

Credit is owed to Jennifer Glacel, LCSW, RPT-S, who contributed greatly to this segment by sharing her expertise on autism.

Religion

Many parents, aunts, uncles, grandparents, and friends can experience an inner conflict between the teachings of their faith and their desire to support the trans person in their life. For some, this may be only a minor struggle, and they find a faith community that embraces diversity and allows them to celebrate their trans family member. Others who may adhere to more conservative religious principles face a much more challenging situation: how to maintain the faith that grounds them and the faith community that supports them, while also loving and supporting their beloved trans family member.

Thoughts from a Therapist ...

I worked with a Muslim family whose trans son no longer wanted to attend the mosque. He explained that it was upsetting to have to pray with women; he wanted to pray with the men of the community. His father, a rather conservative man who was struggling with his child's male gender identity, ultimately concluded that it was more important for his child to continue to attend the mosque. He spoke to the Aman, who granted permission for his son to pray in the area designated for men.

It is true that there are many people who condemn gender diversity in the name of religion, and there are many places of worship where trans youth and their families do not feel welcome. However, I also know of temples, synagogues, and churches that are welcoming to the LGBTQ+ community. Some even engage in significant efforts of outreach to the community. A trans person, or their family, might need to look for a more welcoming community, but they do not have to forfeit worship altogether.

All major world religions worship a supreme being who is called by many different names but is believed to be the Creator of all. With this in mind, it's interesting to consider what creation suggests about gender diversity. When we begin to look, we find dozens of examples of gender diversity in nature. In fact, according to a November 14, 2022, piece by Laura Camón in *El País*, nearly 5 percent of animals have the ability to change their sex.[4]

Many fish, including the well-recognized clown fish made famous by the movie *Finding Nemo*, are hermaphrodites. (This is an acceptable term in reference to fish, but not humans). A school of clownfish is predominantly male but headed by a female. When the female head fish dies, one of the males changes sex to become the new leader of the school.

Male sea horses carry the young. Male penguins are responsible for incubating the eggs until they hatch. Male red-sided garter snakes are able to emit female pheromones. On a reserve in Botswana, several lionesses were discovered to have grown manes and learned to hunt and roar in ways generally reserved for male lions. The examples go on.

Regardless of your specific religion or faith, consider setting aside the concern that gender diversity is wrong in the eyes of the Creator because we have plenty of evidence to the contrary.

---

4   Laura Camón, "Animals that change sex: How and why do they do it?" *El País.* November 14, 2022, https://english.elpais.com/science-tech/2022-11-14/animals-that-change-sex-how-and-why-do-they-do-it.html

Roses And Roaches

I WENT INTO MY SON'S ROOM THIS MORNING to make sure it was ready for the crew who would come to clean the house later that day. Dried roses and leaves littered the carpet in front of his bed, and a new terrarium had appeared on his dresser. I paused, unsure of how to proceed, then sent him a text.

"Are the roses and leaves on your carpet important to you?" I asked.

"No," he answered.

"Okay," I replied. "I will clean them up this time, but from now on, I expect you to pick the debris off your carpet before you leave the house on cleaning days. It's not the ladies' job to do that."

"Yes, ma'am," he answered.

I took a deep breath before posing the next question. "Are there animals living on your dresser?" I asked.

"They are roaches," he answered. "They are safe and clean. I bought them at the Petco in town."

As I tried to process this information, he told me that their names are Cain and Lilith; they cannot fly and do not infest houses; he has been feeding them bananas but is thinking of switching to apples because bananas get mushy too fast; and his self-led science class project is to see what conditions make them the most active. No, he did not get permission from my husband before bringing them into the house.

I took some more deep breaths. "I am not pleased that you bought insects and brought them into your room without getting our permission," I said. "Please do not purchase any more animals of any species and bring them into the house without prior permission. Also, no more roaches. These two may not have successors."

He responded that they only reproduce under certain conditions, and he will not create those.

"You may not buy any more either," I said.

PARENTING TRANS TEENAGERS (or any teenager, really) amounts to constant exposure to roses and roaches, and the questions they provoke. Are the dried roses in a vase on his desk from his sixteenth birthday a reminder of how much he is loved and valued? Why were some of them strewn in front of his bed? Did he need a symbolic barrier to help him sleep at night, as he struggles with insomnia? Was he shooting a photo essay and wanted the image of the dried flowers and leaves against the neutral carpet? Did he put them there as an homage to springtime? Was he distressed or angry and grabbed the ones he could reach out of the vase and threw them on his floor while he sobbed or screamed? He may choose to tell me at dinner tonight, or we may never say another word about it. I may see dried flowers on his carpet every time I go into his room from now on, or it might never happen again.

What if he had asked for permission before buying the roaches? Cain and Lilith would never have made it through the front door. Should I be concerned that the child who cannot remember to water the single plant in his room might kill the roaches with neglect? Or does he desperately need live animals of his own to care for? How much do I care about the banana that turned black and mushy by the sink for the last three days, now that I know it was being used as roach food? If he will sneak roaches into our home, what else might he be sneaking in without my knowledge? How concerned should I be about that?

As parents, we love our trans teens, and we want them to be safe in the world. That's why we are always questioning. Are they safe? Is their depression and anxiety appropriately medicated and treated with therapy? Can they handle the bumps in the road, being more vulnerable than most and encountering even more obstacles to their own becoming than their "typical" peers? Are we giving them enough support? Are we giving them enough space? Do they have enough friends? Do they have the right friends? Do they cry at night over our misuse of pronouns? Do they know how hard we are trying and how much we care?

I read a quote by Elizabeth Stone before I had my children: "Making the decision to have a child—it is momentous. It is to decide forever to have your heart go walking around outside your body." When the children turn out to be trans, they don't just take your heart with them. They take your brain, your peace of mind, your peacekeeping, your diplomacy, and your advocacy too. You can try to retain parts of those for yourself and your work and the other people and things that need your attention, but in the end, your children get the best of you. That is what parenting is all about.

So we learn to take deep breaths before we open bedroom doors because we do not know what will await us on the other side. Today it was roses and roaches. Tomorrow it may be maca-roni and mice. There may be more text messages and more "Yes, ma'am's and more lies about having taken medication this morning—but if my trans teens reach adulthood with a sense of who they are and how much they are loved, the roses and roaches are all worthwhile.

—Valerie Banks Amster

Leaving A Lifetime

I DIDN'T KNOW GAY PEOPLE EXISTED 'til gay marriage was legalized when I was fourteen and my parents sat me down to explain why "those people" were going to hell. I'll never forget driving past a pride flag in California, feeling so sad for them because, in my little heart, I cared about everyone.

The first crush I ever had on a girl was at summer camp when I was thirteen and she held my hand. It felt like I was electrified as I tried to avoid her eyes, blushing. I had no words for what I was experiencing and made myself forget it 'til I remembered in therapy.

When I was fifteen, after being told for years that my twin was in therapy for reasons I would be scarred to know, my now sister sat me down and explained how she was tempted to "cross-dress." We cried. I told her when we turned eighteen, I'd take her to buy her first dress.

When I was seventeen, I went to a Christian university because that was always the only option. I dropped out two years later when I was nineteen because the pressure of trying to be like them as I learned more about myself was crippling. I asked my friends, "Do you think I could be bi?" I was told if I came out, I would ruin the lives of countless kids my family ministered to.

When I was twenty-one, in the height of the pandemic, I had no choice but to return to that same Christian college. My first girlfriend helped me move into my dorm, and I cried.

When I was twenty-two, my school began its witch hunt against the queer community. I knew people who were expelled for being trans, and some of my friends were sent to conversion therapy. People were terrified—I was terrified. The underground gay-straight alliance we had was doxed and dissolved, leaving countless queer kids on campus with no means to find each other for safety and support.

When I was twenty-three, two weeks before my graduation, I got an email informing me I was having a disciplinary meeting. Someone had found my social media and reported it to the school. Mysteriously, a week later, the meeting was canceled. I wore a rainbow dress to my graduation, terrified to do more. I kissed my ex-girlfriend on the cheek posing for a picture in front of the chapel, my knuckles white from holding my diploma so tight that no one could rip it from my hands.

When I was twenty-four, I came out. My whole body shook as I waited for my words to upload. I had always thought my coming out would be bright and cheerful. Instead, I was told, "God would bring me back to the truth I once knew," but for once, I knew my truth. This was affirmed when my newfound community rallied around me to defend me from the hatred, took me in when I was homeless, and saw ME.

They want to erase us. They say they hate the sin and love the sinner as they silently watch us die. And the reason is that we make them uncomfortable because we are different, and they could never be. And that is our superpower. You can't cage us or box us. We are infinite. In the end, I found being queer is the most sacred thing I've ever known.

—Moon

Not Just Another Hospital Stay

I EXPERIENCED MY FIRST SUICIDAL THOUGHTS before I was even in middle school. I cut myself for the first time before I was even in seventh grade. I attempted suicide before I was even in high school. I was just about to finish eighth grade, the third time I was hospitalized for suicidal ideation.

I was fourteen years old and doing virtual school when I told my mom I had planned out my death. At this point, I had already attempted once and been hospitalized twice. My mom took this confession seriously, so we packed a bag and rode over to the nearest hospital. First, we waited for a room. When I got to a room, I had my vitals taken and then waited for a doctor. After sharing my life story with this doctor, I waited for a psychiatrist. When a psychiatrist finally showed up, he told us there were no open beds in the psych units, so I waited for a bed.

All that waiting brought a pathetic realization, "I'm not as important to people as I think." The nurses didn't look at my chart long enough to see that I use a different name or that I use they/them pronouns; they didn't have the capacity for me. And there my mom was, across the tiny white room, her eyes red from crying. It would have been one thing if I came out as gay because it would be years before I could be in a serious relationship; my parents would have had time to process. But being trans, with no option to pretend that I wasn't, meant my parents had little time to adjust to my gender diversity.

We spent the night in the emergency room, tossed and turned, and were woken up in the middle of the night for a blood draw. Finally, in the morning, over twelve hours after arriving, they offered me a bed in the adolescent unit in the hospital.

Wait! The adolescent unit?! The last two times I was in the children's unit! It can't be that different, right?

A nurse pushed me over to the psychiatric building accompanied by a security guard. I was transported in a wheelchair that I didn't need or ask for. I made a joke along the way about getting a punch card for hospital visits. The nurse laughed, even though she had probably heard that one before. Besides, my three total visits must have seemed minuscule compared to the number of times some of the other kids had been there.

Once in the psychiatric building, we rolled past the game room, past the gym area, past the art room, and past the music room until we reached the door that needed a key card to enter the unit.

Oh!

I quickly identified several differences between the children's and adolescents' units. Other than a different overall layout, there was a meeting-type room and a calm-down-type room.

Bathrooms were locked and located in the hallways rather than in the individual rooms and ... two dayrooms instead of one. A girls' dayroom and a boys' dayroom.

Fuuuuuuuuuuck!!!

I was going to have to pick. After a long, restless night and too many hours in the emergency room, there was no chance I could keep it together.

I'd been out as trans for a year at that point and had avoided "Boy or Girl?" "He or She?" "Mr. or Ms.?" at all costs. But this time, I could no longer avoid it. In that moment, with that one choice, one request, one *PICK!* my world was over.

In the end, it wasn't the world-wrecking decision I thought it would be. I started in the girls' dayroom because it felt safer. Later, I got sick of being with the girls and requested to be in the boys' dayroom, although I told the staff I wanted to change because I was constantly referred to as one of the "ladies." During the two weeks I spent there, that was the moment I remember. It's engraved into me.

Having to pick between a girls' dayroom and a boys' dayroom in a psychiatric unit is what life looks like for trans kids. This is what we look like.

—Ray

Statistic

I'm glad my humanity is not adequate
So glad that I'm just another speck
Within the statistic
/sarcastic
Sadistic
When it takes 40% for you to see it
Maybe recognize it
Not yet get it
God forbid support it
Or do
The damage has been done
We've learned that
In turn that
Internalize that
Hope that
We don't copy that
The odds don't look good though
We probably all do it though
They say the data says 42 though
It's more

—Jay

To Those Who Pray

THOSE WHO PRAY ARE AFRAID of my "disease." They give whoever "has it" dirty looks and clutch Bibles that are more dangerous than loaded guns. They are as clueless as they are ignorant.

But I know better. I know that we have no sickness. I know that my best friend, Dezi, is not the deranged person they say he is. He has shown me compassion and ardency. He has shown me intelligence that is rare in the ages of adolescence and adults alike. I know that the real disease is religious ignorance that spreads faster than the rumors at the beauty salon, filled with the same church ladies who spoke in tongues. These ladies attend church, bringing in children who have sewn mouths—just like us. I know that the priests have as much power as they have money and will say or do anything to keep it that way. They will spit quotes as sharp as shiny pocketknives and force us down on our knees 'til they're bleeding. I guess we all have something to be afraid of.

Let it be because they "disagree." Let it be because of the lack of understanding. Let our existence be a conundrum, whether they hate us or the burden of loving us. Let it be because God "doesn't make mistakes." Whatever the reason was to forget

Leelah Alcorn, Semaj Billingslea, Martasia Richmond, or Asher Garcia, at least the Lord will keep *them* warm. So, I know that with one swift motion of a knife against my throat, a bullet through my chest, or a noose around my neck, they will not remember me either.

—Nile

A Journey But So Much More

WHEN A TEEN FIRST IDENTIFIES AS TRANSGEN-DER and starts transitioning emotionally, socially, and medically toward the gender or non-binary state they identify with, it is said that they have "started their gender journey." In the beginning, I thought that using the term journey as a metaphor for what my child, and by extension, our whole family, was beginning was an interesting idea. A nice way of describing the adventure of sorts that lay ahead of us. But I would soon learn just how naive or misguided I was in my impression that this would be a "journey."

Within a year of our teen revealing to us his transgender status, I could see that "journey" was much too mild and friendly a term for what we had experienced so far. Out of curiosity, and some doubts about the adequacy of the word, I looked up the definition of "journey" in my old *Webster's Unabridged*—yes, I still have that tome on my bookcase with its dog-eared pages, highlighted vocabulary words, and a few pressed flowers. I found the following: "a traveling from one place to another, usually taking a long time," "a trip," "a distance, course or area traveled or suitable for travel," and "passage or progress from one stage to another." The listed synonyms included "excursion," "jaunt," "tour," and "roam."

Excursion! Jaunt! Tour! Nothing could be further from the truth, from my perspective. We had only been on this road for a year, and I could tell you that it had been anything but an excursion or jaunt. An excursion, in my mind, is when you decide to get off the interstate highway and take the local roads to meander through the small towns, take in a meal at a Main Street café, stop at the roadside farmers market, or look for treasures at an old antiques shop. And a tour, well, that just hadn't captured our experience so far at all—a tour is when there's at least one person who not only knows what the destination is but how to get there.

When our teen first came out to my husband and me, we did what I'm sure all or most parents do in that situation. We searched the Internet intensely for information on how to be supportive of our kid as he navigated through this new world. We found articles, books, and videos. At the time, we were also fortunate that our teen was already seeing a therapist for his anxiety and depression. The therapist was working closely with a doctor to manage medications in an effort to alleviate the impact of our son's anxiety and depression on his ability to function at home and at school. Our teen was three-quarters through a challenging freshman year at a new school due to those conditions and his learning differences. However, he did have what seemed to be a solid, if small, friend group who were supportive of his gender identity. In fact, he came out to his friends before he told us.

The strength of that friend support was more evident when our son announced that he was going to email the school head and counselors about his gender identity, pronoun preference, and new name—he did not want us to do it; he wanted to do it on his own. I cannot imagine a teen doing that without the knowledge of a supportive and accepting peer group by his side.

So far, there have been a few new twists in the road for us to navigate since his coming out, like remembering to use the new pronoun and name and coaching extended family to be consistent in doing the same. And there was the awkwardness of the first shopping trip to purchase clothes that fit his gender identity—shirts, shoes, underwear, pants, wallet, belt. But our son took most of this in stride; he had a new air of self-assurance that, by extension, boosted my confidence that we could all manage this process together. Nevertheless, these were not by any means simple changes or adjustments that could be made in a matter of days; it took quite a bit of work to make these changes part of our daily routine.

While our family was adjusting to these changes and feeling confident that we would be able to navigate this "journey," we were thrown a curve when our son's therapist announced she was closing her practice. Thus began a long series of disappointing, confusing, and frustrating experiences with various mental health and medical providers.

Over the course of the next year, our son struggled to attend school due to debilitating dysphoria and anxiety. He underwent psychological testing, worked with several different therapists and psychiatrists, and genuinely tried to overcome his anxiety and depression. My husband and I were given a wide range of diagnoses, including dissociative identity disorder, severe anxiety, post-traumatic stress disorder, and autism. The advice we received varied so dramatically that it was exasperating.

One therapist suggested that our son was "playing us," and another questioned whether he was really transgender. One therapist told us to place our son in residential treatment at the same time that another suggested moving forward with medical transition. Both could make a compelling case, and we were left to make significant decisions without a professional consensus. Finding the right psychiatrist to manage medications proved to be equally challenging and required persistence in following up on emails and phone messages that had been unanswered.

Along the way, we had small successes, such as finding a parent education and support program and enrolling our son in a virtual therapy group with other trans teens. However, the school struggles and mental health challenges continued to mount. At the time of this writing, we have a solid team of professionals in place, and even with this solid team of experts, we continue to struggle as a family with the burden of trying to prioritize the various needs: physical, social, academic, and mental health.

I look back on the early days, and the references to a gender journey, and I scoff. It is a journey, yet it is much more than that. It's an adventure, yet not really as entertaining as what that word implies. All in all, it's more of an odyssey—a series of challenges, some met with success and others with failure, temporary setbacks, and U-turns followed by meaningful advances.

It is an odyssey that will strengthen your resolve, test your endurance, and ultimately leave you with the realization that you are stronger than you ever imagined—and you will do anything to protect your child. An odyssey in which there can be moments of confusion, self-doubt, and perhaps even a touch of despair, but in turn, can also bring enlightenment and strength to all who accept the challenge of accompanying their loved one on this "journey."

—Juli

Looking
Forward

Just Embrace

We should live to the beat of one drum.
Human
We should dance to the rhythm of one heart.
Not apart.
Together.
Like the root tips of groves touching like toes.
Maple and oak branches entwining like fingers around that rose.
Love knows.

Love forgives.
Intention, effort,
mean everything.
And that old, weathered branch,
mistaken for dead?
Blossoming.

Just embrace.

Excerpt taken from *Just Embrace* by Rula Sinara

WHAT DOES THE FUTURE LOOK LIKE regarding our acceptance of gender diversity? It depends on how far into the future we look. Most likely the current backlash against progress will continue for some time, and conditions may even get a little worse before they get better. It is hard to imagine anything worse than a ban on gender-affirming care in over thirteen states in our country, but major shifts in the way people think always take time.

However, history assures us that a positive shift *will* happen.

Throughout history, we see that major shifts in paradigm are never popular when first presented. There was a time when intelligent and educated people believed sincerely that the world was flat. To suggest otherwise was considered absurd, and those who set off to prove it were called crazy. There was a time when the suggestion that the world revolved around the sun (and not the other way around) was deemed heresy. These were significant shifts in paradigm. They challenged our sense of what we felt was known ... and what was right. To allow ourselves to think differently about something we have believed to be true is difficult. And it is especially difficult for those who are more invested in the status quo than for those who are not.

As described earlier, one hundred years ago, a shift in paradigm occurred when it was ultimately determined that left-handedness was *not* a sign of the devil. The current increase in those coming out as trans and non-binary is similar to the rapid increase in left-handedness we saw in the 1920s to 1940s. During that time, acceptance grew for individuals to use their left hand when that was more natural for them.

Many who read this book might remember the Civil Rights Movement and the paradigm shift that was required to understand that persons of color were not inferior and should have equal opportunities and legal rights in our country. And the women's rights movement of the 1960s and 1970s involved another paradigm shift in the roles and capabilities of women. The gay rights movement was another paradigm shift for people, some of whom genuinely believed that gays and lesbians were "sick" and needed conversion therapy. Today, that is a minority opinion and one that is not upheld in the courts.

Our youth today are demanding a new paradigm shift around gender diversity. And, as history would predict, there are those who are vehemently opposed to it. Paradigm shifts are often perceived as threatening and not made easily. However, progress is never stopped. It might be slowed and detoured, but as described above, throughout history, paradigm shifts have prevailed. Today, no one questions that the world is round and that it revolves around the sun. Most of us now believe that people of color, women, and gays are all equal and deserve the same rights.

One day, we will look back at the current reaction to gender diversity and feel as foolish as we do when considering that we once naively thought the world was flat. Many will look back with shame at how trans individuals are currently being treated, similar to the shame we carry at having once tolerated slavery.

We cannot predict when this paradigm shift will happen, but we can be confident that it will. One day, generations will scoff at the ignorance and naiveté that ever suggested there was a binary and that gender diversity was anything other than a wonderful variation in our humanity.

THAT QUEER AND TRANS INDIVIDUALS ARE THE BRAVEST PEOPLE FOR DOING THE LIFESAVING WORK FOR DISCOVERING, BEING, AND LIVING AT OUR MOST AUTHENTIC AND TRUE SELF IN A WORLD THAT EVERY DAY SEEKS TO ERASE US

IT'S NOT A MENTAL ILLNESS; IT'S A DEEPER UNDERSTANDING OF ONESELF AND THE COURAGE TO NOT LIVE AS SOMETHING YOU AREN'T

THAT IT REALLY SUCKS SOMETIMES, BUT WE CAN'T CHANGE IT

YOU DON'T HAVE TO BE TRANS TO FREE YOURSELF FROM GENDER NORMS AND EXPECTATIONS. TRANS LIBERATION IS YOUR LIBERATION TOO

WE ARE PEOPLE TOO

HOW DIFFICULT IT IS TO ACCESS GENDER-AFFIRMING CARE

What do you wish more cisgendered people knew/ understood?

I WISH THEY KNEW HOW MUCH IT HURTS TO BE MISGENDERED

HOW HARD IT REALLY IS AND THAT I NEVER CHOSE THIS

NOT ALL TRANS PEOPLE ARE THE SAME

YOUR SUPPORT MATTERS MORE THAN YOU MIGHT REALIZE, AND IT CAN HELP CREATE A MORE COMPASSIONATE AND UNDERSTANDING WORLD FOR ALL OF US

THE IMPORTANCE OF VALIDATION AND RESPECT FOR OUR GENDER IDENTITY. IT'S NOT A PHASE OR A CHOICE; IT'S AN INTRINSIC PART OF WHO WE ARE

CIS IS NOT A SLUR, AND ME BEING TRANS DOESN'T HARM YOU OR ANYONE

TRANS EXISTENCE HAS NOTHING TO DO WITH YOU. LEAVE US ALONE TO LIVE OUR LIVES IN PEACE

EVERYONE SHOULD HAVE MORE FUN WITH GENDER

TO YOU, SOMETHING MIGHT NOT BE A BIG DEAL, BUT TRANS PEOPLE HAVE TO DEAL WITH 100 THINGS A DAY THAT "AREN'T A BIG DEAL." WE'RE NOT OVERREACTING, WE'RE TIRED. SOMEONE HITTING YOU WITH A PILLOW ONCE IS INNOCUOUS, BUT SOMEONE HITTING YOU WITH A PILLOW 100 TIMES HURTS A LOT. AND THAT'S NOT EVEN MENTIONING THE PEOPLE CARRYING BRICKS

Fighting For The Future

I THINK I WILL ALWAYS QUESTION the way I stand, sit, talk, write, and dress. I'm always wondering if what I'm doing is "too feminine" and if I'm being perceived as a woman. Realistically, I know there is no such thing as a "feminine" way to stand, sit, talk, write, or dress. Having said that, I've worn the same cargo shorts every summer since I was twelve because I believed they were "masculine." I think I wear them more out of fear than comfort. Fear of rejection, of how others will perceive me, of stereotypes and hatred.

I don't know if I will ever feel one hundred percent confident and comfortable in my skin, but I do know that being on testosterone and having top surgery have significantly improved my well-being. Though, even after being out for five years, I don't tell my coworkers or classmates about my identity, out of fear of being alienated by them. It seems that having people know who I am, and purposely destroying all sense of confidence I have in myself, is far worse than simply being rejected or ignored. In the former, they've taken my greatest sense of self and used it to hurt me, and others like me. I'm not necessarily ashamed of who I am but more afraid of how I'll be perceived by those around me.

Considering the political climate surrounding the topic of LGBTQ+ rights in this country, I've thought many times about moving elsewhere in the world. Somewhere not only accepting, which implies only tolerance, but loving and welcoming as well. As I thought about leaving, though, I remembered that once an idea is shared, in this case, queer hatred, it doesn't stop, even after the initial mind of this idea has passed. Meaning, running from the problem will not solve it. The idea will take much longer to spread to other countries and continents, but once it reaches other like minds, who knows how far it will travel? Though the idea of standing up for myself is an unnerving one, I try to remember that it's really not only me I'm fighting for. It's all the people who have yet to experience true queer joy, for future generations, and for the discouraged. We all deserve life, safety, happiness, freedom, and love.

—Max Gifford

It Won't Happen Overnight

It won't happen overnight
But we will fight
For the rights
Of those beaten, broken down
On the ground and
Surround them with love
We'll shove the dove above
Into the light
We'll fight for peace
We won't be polite to police
For the beastime of us people
With our might we increase
The peaceful peacetime
We unite like the spaceflight
For what's right every weeknight
Past sunlight
We shine bright at night as we fight
We handwrite a piece of our minds

To decrease the police and the hate

That we face every date

Is it our fate to carry the weight

Of minority death rates

We have so much on our plates

Yet you treat us that we must have a low body weight

Escape

You say

Be straight

Jacket

You say we're insane

We feel so much pain

Our name is the bane of your existence

We help each other out

Help us obtain and gain

No matter how hard the rain is in our brain

You've painted us payment

The paining pavement

You've rolled out in front of us

We have to be the blunt of us

And confront the constant current events

This moment is moving with urgent meaning

Seeing that it hadn't it hasn't it haven't it shouldn't it couldn't it

needn't it wouldn't turn around

For silence is its own vacant defendant

Enforcement and acknowledgment of a broken sight

Yes we will fight for our rights

No it won't happen overnight

But it will happen with unity's might

—Jay

When Tomorrow Comes

WHEN TOMORROW COMES, *I will feel the prickle of the foggy Oakland air meet*
my skin, stretch my arms to the gray sky, and sigh—I'm lucky to be alive.

I'm a man of trans experience; a twenty-seven-year-old real-live trans adult. I'm also a dog dad, a creator, an athlete, a softball coach, a friend, a chosen uncle, an award-winning educator, and so much more. For so long, all of these things were just dreams that felt entirely out of my reach ...

I grew up in an incredibly transphobic household. The people who brought me into this world drilled shame into me like time-tables. They constantly denied my reality, threatened me, and destroyed my self-esteem, and I internalized their hatred until it was as automatic as arithmetic. I spent so many years of life believing that a happy future was out of the question for me as a trans person. Some days, those thoughts still ring loudly in my brain, but when I pause, I see the truth: I've become living proof to the contrary.

Years of medical transition, deep inner work, and estrangement from my abusive family have allowed me to be present in my body and my life, fully and authentically, for the first time. I have never felt so alive. Despite my obvious signs of life, my parents choose to believe that their child is dead. They would rather have a dead daughter than a happy, thriving, living trans son.

At four, I was diagnosed with gender identity disorder. My parents were adamant that no daughter of theirs would ever be a "lesbian," and thus began years of (unsuccessful) conversion therapy.

At thirteen, when I finally re-found the words and courage to live my truth after having it shoved down, I was met with "don't tell anyone at school; they will all hate you."

At fifteen, I got "you are disgusting" as my chest binders were cut up and all access to the outside world was cut off.

At sixteen, my mother screamed, "I will kill myself if you medically transition, and my suicide will be your fault."

At twenty, I finally gathered the strength to choose myself and started hormones after previously resigning to a morbid fate. I was immediately off the health insurance, out of the will, bribed to detransition, and sent death threats.

At twenty-two, I discovered that my mother was behind a widely followed anti-trans social media account and ran a "gender critical" parent support network, where parents swapped tips on how to abuse their trans children into cisness. The day I was under the knife for top surgery, she was raising money to push an anti-trans bathroom bill forward in my state.

It's a strange experience to reach an age you didn't think you'd see; to become the person you so desperately needed but never had nor expected to exist. At the same time, being myself, in all of my multitudes, is incredibly natural, and existing on this Earth finally feels right. When I look in the mirror, I see—physically and psychically—the person I used to daydream about while crying myself to sleep.

When tomorrow comes, I will bear my scars and bare my soul. Chills running down my spine, I'll thank teenage me for keeping me earthside.

As a teen, I wanted so badly to move away from my conservative East Coast hometown and settle in San Francisco. I was desperate for community and felt deeply drawn to the vision of freedom with other people like me. I'd spend hours online trying to figure out how to make this happen for myself, how to find trans people living happy lives. I remember coming across some summer camps for trans kids online and immediately sobbing because I knew that was way out of the realm of possibility for me. Well, over a decade later, and I'm now living out many of the dreams I had as a teen. Just to name a few: I moved to California, my body looks more and more like my own every day, and I'm a counselor at a camp for trans kids!

There's something truly magical about sharing space with 150 trans kids and a staff of trans adults. Every morning at check-in, as I watched parents drop off their children at trans camp, I witnessed so much love. There were the expected hugs and summer-camp-smiles, but what really struck me were the parents using their child's chosen names and new pronouns. This love opened my heart and inspired me to push out past the deeply internalized shame and share my story.

When tomorrow comes, I will see myself in the next generation—I will know their pain and I will feel their joy. I'm the person I needed when I was a boy.

At the end of the camp week, we held a closing ceremony with all of the kids' parents in attendance. Shortly before we brought the kids in to sing a song, I walked up on stage in an auditorium packed with parents, and I shared some anecdotes from my life. I ended with, "Thank you for loving your trans kids." Some parents cried when they heard the ways I had suffered, and many lined up to give me hugs while thanking me for existing. "You deserved parents who loved you," these near-strangers said, holding me in an embrace. "We love you." They may have hardly known me, but I saw the way the camp parents love their trans kids, and I know they're sincere.

My mother still chooses to believe that I was "taken by the trans cult." If this is what the trans cult looks like—a roomful of loving parents cheering on their trans children, not despite their transness but, in this case, because of it—then so be it. It would have absolutely changed my life if I'd had an opportunity to be in a community like this as a kid or teen, and I am deeply grateful to be a part of it now.

Everything I do is only possible because teenage-me stayed alive, and I am so grateful for him. I survived my teen years (and all the other ones) against all odds and expectations—because of the trans people who shared their stories and showed me that life could exist for me, the mentors who showed up for me, the chosen family I built, and the tenacity of a young person dying to finally live. Trans kids deserve to grow up, and every act of support helps that happen.

> *When tomorrow comes, I will swim and flow, bare-chested with pride, and be grateful I survived; basking in the beauty of this trans life.*

—Owen Dempsey

Our Invitation
to You

THANK YOU FOR READING *Trans Anthology Project.* We are hopeful you learned some things you didn't know before. We trust you were impacted by the stories, poems, and quotes from those who responded to our online survey. And we hope you were able to empathize with the challenges faced by those in the transgender community.

So, now, we invite you to get involved in supporting the rights of trans persons. There is a divide in our country between those who recognize that trans persons are human and deserve all the rights and protections afforded to anyone else and those who seem to vilify and persecute the entire population of trans youth and adults. The trans community needs the support of people like YOU.

There are numerous ways that you can be an ally to the trans community, and many of them are rather easy and simple to do.

- Allow *yourself* the paradigm shift to see gender as non-binary and encourage others to do the same.
- Challenge ignorance and prejudice when you hear it.
- Be kind to trans persons in your workplace, school, or community.
- Donate to organizations that are working to secure rights for trans persons.
- Give a copy of *Trans Anthology Project* to someone you know.
- Continue to educate yourself by reading books and watching videos or documentaries.
- Follow the Trans Anthology Project on Instagram to help spread awareness.

With deepest gratitude,
Heather and Chrissy

Trans Anthology Project Surveys

FROM MARCH THROUGH OCTOBER 2023, the Trans Anthology Project hosted two anonymous online surveys: one for trans and non-binary teens and young adults and one for parents of trans and non-binary teens and young adults.

The surveys have allowed us to add almost 150 more voices to *Trans Anthology Project*. Of these voices, roughly 60 percent are from trans and non-binary teens and young adults, with the remaining 40 percent of voices from parents of trans and non-binary teens and young adults.

The survey was primarily advertised on our Instagram account, as well as through Heather's clinical practice newsletter and hosted on TypeForm. Unless otherwise noted, all snippets throughout the book were sourced from these survey results.

Teen Survey

A total of eighty-six unique trans and non-binary teens and young adults completed the survey. Teen participants ranged in age, with the vast majority being fifteen or older. The gender identities of respondents also varied, though respondents predominantly identified as transgender or non-binary.

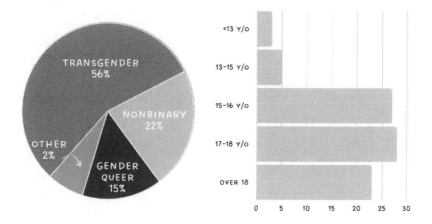

Q: *How old were you when you first began to suspect that your gender identity was different from the one assigned to you at birth?*

Most respondents reported that they first suspected something between the ages of twelve and fifteen years old, with almost as many reporting between the ages of six and eleven years old. About a handful reported an early inkling, between the ages of birth and five years old, as well as between the ages of sixteen and eighteen years old. One respondent reported attuning to their gender difference beyond the age of eighteen.

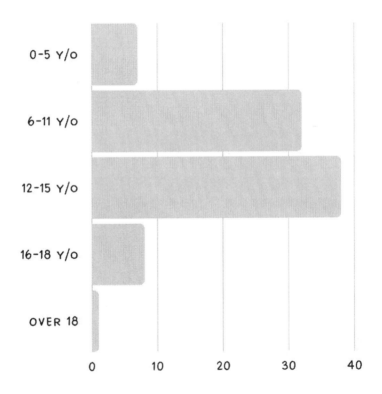

Q: **How long did you wait before telling someone about your transgender or non-binary identity?**

As the numbers show above, most respondents (60 percent) reported that they first told at least one other person about their transgender or non-binary identity within the first six months of being aware of it themselves. An additional 30 percent waited one to two years, with the remaining 10 percent waiting longer.

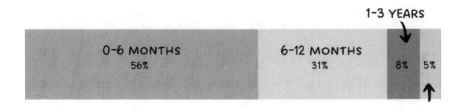

Q: **In what settings are you currently out?**

As mentioned earlier in the book, coming out is a highly personalized experience that is often based on many forces in a teen's life, both tangible and intangible. As a result, they may not be "out" in all settings all at once. For example, while roughly three-quarters of our respondents reported being "out" to their immediate family, less than 50 percent reported being "out" to extended family. While 70 percent reported being "out" at school, only 60 percent reported being "out" at extracurricular activities, including sports.

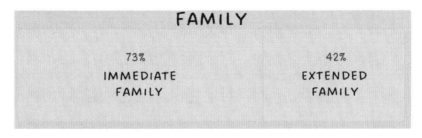

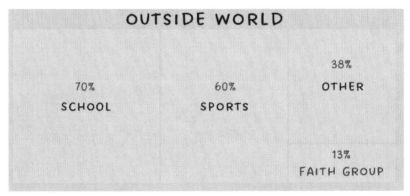

"Other" settings noted: specific friends, online spaces, work, medical providers, and drag community.

Q: *Have you begun transition? If so, what levels(s)?*

Transitioning is as highly personalized a part of a gender journey as any other. In addition, not all transgender, non-binary, and queer people will want to transition, are able to transition, or feel the need to transition across all three levels (social, medical, and legal). For example, almost all respondents to our survey reported that they have socially transitioned to some extent (name, pronouns, and appearance), while far less, 36 percent, reported having begun medical transition. Several respondents reported having the desire to pursue medical transition in the future, while others were currently satisfied as is. Even fewer respondents reported having pursued any legal transition as of yet.

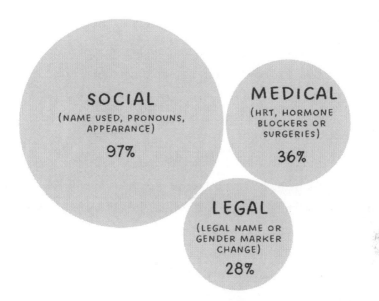

SOCIAL
(NAME USED, PRONOUNS, APPEARANCE)
97%

MEDICAL
(HRT, HORMONE BLOCKERS OR SURGERIES)
36%

LEGAL
(LEGAL NAME OR GENDER MARKER CHANGE)
28%

Q: **What has been the hardest part of your gender journey?**

- All the *legislation has scared me immensely, and the random people that wish me dead just because of something that is out of my control.*
- *Accepting that no matter how much I wish I was, I'm not a cis girl.*
- *Learning who's accepting and who's not.*
- *Realizing that I had to sacrifice many important teenage experiences because I was transgender. While my peers were enjoying their adolescence, I often had to put my safety above my desire to fit in. It was heartbreaking to watch from the sidelines, knowing that I couldn't fully participate in activities I longed to be a part of.*
- *My parents' reaction for sure. And continuing to navigate healthcare and legal systems with only some of my documents changed.*

- *Coming out to myself was extremely difficult. I had a lot of internalized transphobia and internalized hatred of men and felt like I was betraying my lesbian and queer woman community by coming out as a man. That was the hardest internal obstacle I had to overcome.*
- *Feeling pressured to put a label on how I identify and having conflicting feelings between wanting to be a girl and wanting to be myself.*
- *Just accepting that there will always be people who refuse to see me for who I am for as long as I live, especially family.*
- *The discrimination and fear of discrimination if the wrong person learns of my gender identity. Not to mention the constant negative press about trans people like me.*
- *Being an outcast has easily been the hardest part. It's really hard to make friends when you're in transition, as you're not quite a man and not quite a woman.*
- *The lack of support.*
- *The hardest part is accepting that I may never look the way I want to. I've already gone through the majority of puberty, and I'm pretty sure there's no way to make my hips magically shrink.*

Q: What has been the best or most rewarding part of your gender journey?

- *Being myself and feeling confident in my identity. I feel like because I had so much to think about, I understand myself better than most people do because I took the time to explore my identity.*
- *Being seen as myself and being able to see myself as I am! Hormones and surgery have made me like what I see in the mirror, and after top surgery, it was the first time ever that I actually felt like I was seeing myself when I looked in the mirror.*

- *Seeing the bright and clear light in my eyes and hearing the strength and joy in my voice, which have come with each act of self-love and each step of becoming my most authentic self.*
- *Getting to be my full and authentic self.*
- *Coming out has taught me a lot of things. I have learned how to stand up for myself, how to push through awkward conversations, and how to make worthwhile friends. I've learned not to base my self-worth on other people's opinions of me.*
- *The most rewarding is finally feeling like I'm becoming my true self and finding a community.*
- *I've loved having my body actually represent me.*

Q: **What was been the most helpful thing your parents have done to support you on your gender journey?**

- *They got me my first binder.*
- *Using my name, going to pride events with me, going to court when I went to protest anti-trans bills, and supporting me in the school system to get my name and gender changed there!*
- *They quit fighting me on it.*
- *Helped me get therapy.*
- *Used my pronouns/name and helped with gender-affirming clothes.*
- *Calling me their son because it feels like they finally see me like that.*
- *They had my back and stood by me being a dude despite social back-lash, and that meant a lot to me.*
- *Finding a therapist specializing in gender who was also trans and helping me get on hormones.*
- *Taking extra caution not to misgender me to my friends from school, with whom I'm stealth.*

- *Helped me join support groups and do various things to involve myself in the LGBTQ+ community.*
- *Helped me get a legal name change.*
- *Advocating for me in school.*
- *Defending me and my pronouns to other family members and to strangers.*
- *Listening and trying to learn from me.*
- *Contributing money to help with HT and surgery.*
- *Going into conversations with an open mind in a heart ready to love, no matter what.*
- *My mom has always been there if I needed to talk.*
- *Taught my baby brother to say my preferred name.*
- *Being able to talk with my mom about everything, both joy and grief.*

Q: What types of comments make you feel UNsupported by your parents?

- Denying that I am trans or non-binary.
  - *"You will always be my little girl ..."*
  - *"You're just trying to fit in ... it's just a phase."*
  - *"Why can't you just be happy the way you are?"*
  - *"Is your OCD causing this?"*

- Justifying their use of incorrect name and pronouns.
  - *"I've known you for so long that it's so hard to adjust!"*
  - *"We spent months choosing that name when you were a baby!"*
  - *"I don't really like your new name."*
  - *"They/them is just too confusing."*

- Trying to talk me out of transitioning.
  - *"Why can't you just be a butch girl?"*
  - *"Why can't you just be normal?"*
  - *"You're ruining yourself."*
  - *"You're not trans enough to need top surgery."*

Q: **How does it make you feel when your parents make unsupportive comments?**

- *It has made me very sad and definitely affected my mental health, and not in a good way.*
- *Makes me feel more distant from them and like they are only accepting of me in a performative way rather than a genuine way.*
- *I don't feel safe in my house to just be me.*
- *It made me feel really hopeless and unloved, knowing my family couldn't put their religion aside and accept me.*
- *It made me feel like I was being hidden, that I was something to be ashamed of that they did not want people to see.*
- *A little trapped and hopeless and suicidal.*

Q: **What advice would you give a young person just starting out on their gender journey?**

- *It will be hard at first, but once you break through the initial hostility and start to thrive as your true self, people will accept you. It's important to find community, especially in the early transition days. Find supportive friends who will affirm you and help you grow into your true gender.*
- *Find a trusted someone to listen to and cheer you on.*

- *You got this. No one knows you and your identity better than you. Don't let anyone else try and convince you otherwise, because they sure as hell will try. But at the end of the day, the only person whose opinion matters is yours.*
- *Let yourself explore. You don't have to land on a label right away (or at all).*
- *Don't feel the need to explain yourself or your identity to anybody. You don't need validation or permission to be and express yourself. Getting to know yourself is a lifelong journey, and you are allowed to change and grow. Others might be welcomed into the process, but no one has the right to inhibit, critique, or influence it in ways you are not comfortable with.*

Parent Survey

Fifty-eight parents responded to our anonymous online survey, the children of whom represented a fairly even distribution of gender identities. The majority of these children came out to their parents during middle and high school.

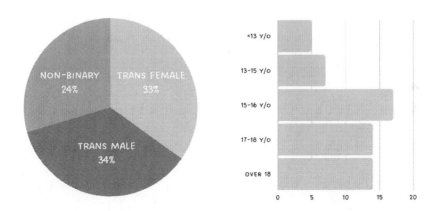

Q: How old was your child when they came out as transgender?

Contrary to the idea popularized in the press, only 10 percent of the respondents to our survey reported that their child was in elementary school or younger when they first came out. The majority of respondents reported that their child came out during middle school, high school, or beyond.

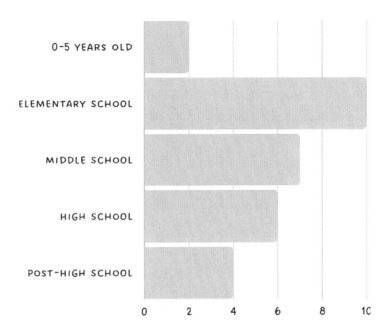

0-5 YEARS OLD

ELEMENTARY SCHOOL

MIDDLE SCHOOL

HIGH SCHOOL

POST-HIGH SCHOOL

0   2   4   6   8   10

Q: **Were you surprised when your child came out? Why or why not?**

Respondents tended to be slightly more surprised than not, with 14 percent in the middle. Some respondents describe being utterly shocked while others saw clues along the way, or at least in hindsight.

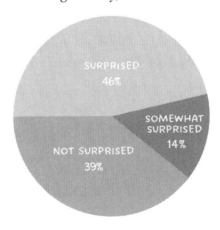

SURPRISED
46%

SOMEWHAT
SURPRISED
14%

NOT SURPRISED
39%

- As gay, no. As trans, yes. It just never crossed my mind that this is where she was headed!
- Not really. We had wondered for a long time if gender identity was challenging for her.
- Yes. As a child, they would only wear dresses and were super into princesses. At the time, we were struggling with COVID and other issues at home, so I thought it was a way for them to reinvent themselves.
- Yes. I didn't feel I had seen any signs at all during the first twelve years. They liked a lesbian at the time, so I thought it was so she would like them back.
- Yes and no—we knew they were exploring gender but didn't realize they were gender fluid.
- Yes. Because they kept it a secret for a long time.
- Not entirely. I remembered many things that made me say, Oh! That could explain certain things.
- Sort of, but in hindsight, it seemed to make sense and explain a bit about his anxiety and depression.
- Shocked. We had no idea.
- Yes, I was definitely surprised. My child was a happy little girl for eleven or twelve years and then she just wasn't. I had to educate myself about what it means to be transgender.
- Yes and no. I think I wanted to handle it better than I did. I worried that I missed signs. I wanted to allow for support of them but not put them into a box of their identity.
- Yes. Never saw anything unusual pre-puberty.
- No, all signs pointed to her being a girl from early childhood. I just knew nothing about being trans.
- Yes. I was very surprised because he never had traditionally male interests, friends, etc.
- No. Because I suspected it by then.

- *Not entirely, I knew there was a feeling/need that was nagging at them and finally they knew what to name it and how to live that feeling.*

Q: When your child came out, which resources were most helpful or unhelpful and why?

- PFLAG, close friends, TRUE Center for Gender Diversity, Gender Spectrum
- *Articles in media on transgender were generally not*
- *Support groups have been helpful*
- *Books*
- *Pediatrician and therapist*
- *Books and therapists; the internet was okay but there is a lot of misinformation*
- *My faith community was not. They were totally unaccepting.*
- *Our church community, as there are trans members of the congregation and there was a lesbian rector at the time.*
- *Support groups, mental health professionals. and books were the most helpful.*
- *Our pediatrician was helpful because she referred us to mental health professionals. She encouraged us to be supportive from the start.*
- *It was hard at first to find a therapist who truly got them. A lot of therapists said they did, but then it turned out they didn't.*
- *Initially I think I had no idea what to even look for. I talked to a different child's therapist and she told me there is nothing wrong with your child. which has continued to resonate today. Figuring out a therapist for my child and being exposed to other parents of trans children has been so helpful. Today, a couple of years in I feel*

like I know better where to look and find appropriate information.

- *The best was a support group of families all going through the same thing. Words cannot describe how huge of a positive impact that was. Being able to share with others who understood the joys and challenges was so special.*

Q: **How easy or difficult was it to begin using new preferred pronouns and names?**

- *A little bit of both. We had ten years of one name and pronouns, so it took some getting used to, but there was never any question about supporting her. There was definitely a grieving process too.*
- *Difficult. I went through a grieving process. Now the name is how I see him, but I still slip on gender occasionally.*
- *Hard at first simply out of habit for using the others.*
- *Personally, we used preferred name but were crushed. After years of using pronouns, I find it hard when speaking. Writing I seem to have somewhat mastered.*
- *The name was easy because it was similar to the birth name and could have been a nickname. Pronouns are hard to remember, and it takes some effort to be mindful in speech. I find older people, neighbors, and relatives struggle with the pronouns.*
- *Very difficult. Just took some getting used to.*
- *The pronouns took more practice than the name change.*
- *It's a work in progress. The grammar fan in me hates how they don't match up!!*
- *Not for me—I'm a language teacher and I don't mind being corrected. My husband, the scientist who always wants to be right had a much harder time.*

- *Very difficult—especially because our immediate family is only using them around certain people. Lots of switching back and forth.*
- *When I was tired or thinking about things from the past I would slip up—mostly with pronouns and a couple times with the name(s) and when they were out at home but not with others—that was so hard to switch back and forth!*
- *It was really difficult. When you have known someone for eleven years and you are used to one thing it is hard to change. But we did change and now it feels weird to think about the given name. The hardest part is always having to explain the new name and pronouns. It's hard that everyone is not accepting.*
- *Yes, only because my child hasn't come out to everyone yet and I need to keep track of when/with which people to use the right pronoun.*

Q: **What gender-affirming treatments has your child pursued at this point in your gender journey?**

Roughly half of respondents reported that their child had not yet pursued medical transition. Those whose children had begun some level of medical transition were more likely to have begun either hormone therapy or hormone blockers, depending on the age of their children.

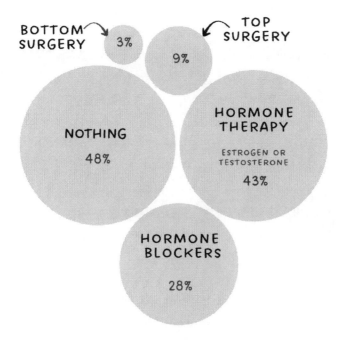

BOTTOM SURGERY 3%

TOP SURGERY 9%

NOTHING 48%

HORMONE THERAPY

ESTROGEN OR TESTOSTERONE

43%

HORMONE BLOCKERS

28%

Q: **What has your experience been trying to find and then work with gender-affirming medical providers?**

- *Wonderful! Thanks to the mom friend with a trans daughter. She has been our spirit guide!!*
- *I do search for them, but we have been lucky in that our providers have been accepting.*
- *My adult child found a great top surgeon (on an internet chat group I think, not really sure). We went together for the appointments, and both of us had a good feeling about his practice. It was a very affirming and good experience. They also found, just by accident, a female gynecologist who specializes in trans care.*
- *Slow process but thankful I am in the part of the country I am in.*
- *Fairly positive*

- It was sooooo hard to find them, but they are fantastic!
- We had a good experience that became awful. The intake coordinator was amazing, but doctor was an overworked old man that has no business being in the field he is in. He wasn't very good at answering our questions. We are now having an amazing experience elsewhere where her doctor is now of the community. She answers our questions and makes a point to ask if we need help with anything. Such a welcoming experience.
- She found them all beginning three years ago. Thank goodness because we are in Texas, and it would be much harder now.
- It's been very positive and quicker than many.

Q: People can say and do hurtful things out of fear or lack of education. What were some of the hurtful things others said or did as they adjusted to your child's gender identity?

- Providing poorly informed "advice" and suggestions. Comments like "I'm sure he will outgrow it!"
- One grandparent has been vocal about how she "doesn't buy" that all these kids are really trans and that they shouldn't be told stories that encourage it in school. I feel the impact of those statements in my guts.
- My sister doesn't understand at all. She thinks I'm being too lenient and that all kids want to change their name and I shouldn't have said yes. She tells me all the time just to be a parent and say no to my kids.
- Anything that was said was not in front of me or my child. Most have been very supportive.
- "Don't do surgery." "It's just a phase." and "It's from too much time on the internet." Then there are my "friends" on Facebook who post

stupid things they think are funny and have no idea I'm the parent of a transgender child. It's hurtful.

- *Refusing to support their pronouns.*
- *Honestly, nothing. People have been supportive.*
- *Some said I was a bad parent and that I was handling this all wrong.*
- *"Is he sure about this?" "Did you do research before allowing any medical treatment?" "Could this be because they experienced some sort of trauma or abuse?"*
- *My MIL thought my child was under the influence of a cult.*
- *They asked inappropriate medical questions.*
- *They simply ignore the requests for correct pronouns—they still do this.*
- *Nothing. We've not yet told anyone who we didn't know would be receptive.*
- *We were told we were abusing our child, that we needed a psych evaluation for "letting" our child do this, that I made my kid a girl for not playing baseball enough, that it will be because of me that they get beat up in school ... the list goes on and on.*
- *I don't think people purposely said unkind things to my child, but they still misgender him on a regular basis.*
- *Kept calling her by her birth name that was assigned at birth instead of her chosen name.*
- *Our family members who were not supportive stayed pretty silent about it, versus saying anything hurtful.*
- *A good friend recently told me that she didn't support trans kids using the boys' bathroom because it wasn't fair to make her son feel uncomfortable and so many other kids just so a few kids could feel better. When I reminded her that these "few" kids were so much more likely to self-harm (she knows my child had attempted suicide) and suffer from depression, she didn't budge at all.*
- *None so far*

- *Our best friends decided to ghost us after our youngest came out to them. We went from at least monthly spontaneous dinner parties, every New Year's Eve spent together, and trips together to having zero contact with them. Thank goodness, our trans son and their daughter are still close friends, but we parents never see each other anymore. Right when lots was going on for us and we needed friends more than ever, they apparently decided their discomfort at how we handled his gender journey was more important than the previous ten years of shared experiences and joys.*
- *Awkward silence from people is one of the worst things one can say. Saying nothing can say so much. I also had family members ask me when was the last time I read the Bible.*
- *My mom told me it was my job as her parent to make sure she knows she has a penis and was a boy.*

Q: What advice would you offer a parent who has just learned that their child is gender diverse?

- *Believe your child. Even if you are losing your mind internally, show them your unconditional love and acceptance.*
- *Take things one day at a time and get support because you need it too.*
- *It's okay. Really, wherever you are with it, it's okay. Be there. Let yourself. And, if you have pain, fear, anger, or worry, address that for yourself with help from someone educated on the topic so you're not bleeding it all over your kiddo. I wish I could go back in time and edit myself.*
- *Beyond the pain and worry (sometimes alongside the pain and worry), it's really a beautiful and fascinating journey.*
- *Just be open and listen to your child. Even if it's not something you agree with, being open will help your child feel like they can talk to you.*

- *Make a safe environment for your child to express feelings and explore it.*

- *Your kid is still the same person with the same strengths, same weaknesses, same motivations and fears. You just know more about who they always were.*

- *It's a marathon, not a sprint, and they will have many indecisive days that you will need to support and understand.*

- *The best advice I ever got was from Joel Baum at Gender Spectrum who said to follow our child's lead. I'm an anxious person anyway and I was trying to plan out her whole future to prepare, and when he said that, it took a lot of that self-imposed pressure off.*

- *Speak with a support group that is supportive of the trans community and has experience in guidance to offer support.*

- *You are allowed to feel unsure and experience grief at the loss of what you expected.*

- *Follow positive trans accounts on Instagram to see the joy.*

- *Be open-minded, accept them, and love them for being who they are.*

- *Find someone to talk to. You will need someone to share your feelings with and learn. I am still crushed over the term deadname.*

- *Be a good listener, accept that this is your child, and focus on having a loving relationship. I wish I had been more accepting from the very beginning and have regrets about how I handled some things, early on.*

- *Put your child first and try to see things from their point of view. There's a poem called "Welcome to Holland" by Emily Perl Kingsley written for parents of children with disabilities that can also apply to parents of transgender kids. Learn as much as you can and find a group of parents in the same boat as you.*

- *Talk to your child.*

- *Join an affirming parent group and get educated.*

- *Know they are the same person they've always been, but let yourself mourn the kid you thought they were and the adult you thought they would become.*
- *Try hard not to think about how it all impacts you or how friends and family will react.*
- *Find someone you can talk with right away. It really helps if you can articulate your feelings out loud.*
- *Take a deep breath every day and just love your child.*
- *Listen to trans people and trust their experience and knowledge.*
- *Be kind to yourself. Give yourself time and seek out the support you need. It's okay to love your child with all your heart and be completely bewildered about what is happening. The better you take care of yourself and find the answers you need the better you can take care of your child.*
- *Your child is the same kid they've always been—just a truer and happier version.*
- *Find your people, other parents. There is an element of grief, and you will need a safe space to express it without exposing your child to it.*
- *Hang in there; it's a bit of a wild ride and will challenge your expectations. However, life is interesting and having a gender-diverse child will open your heart and mind to many possibilities.*

Q: **What do you wish more cisgender people understood about your child and/or the entire trans community?**

- *So many are hurting and vulnerable. Trans people just want to make their way in the world.*
- *Being a trans person is not really a choice; it is allowing the person to be who they really are.*
- *That what's in their pants is none of your damn business.*

- *Members of the trans community are not really different from anyone else—they are people, brothers, sisters, moms, dads, cousins, friends, etc. Maybe they dress a little funny sometimes, but hey, take a look at some high school yearbooks from the 70s and 80s and then tell me about funny clothes and hairstyles!*

- *They are human. They are amazing. They are no different from anyone else.*

- *It's not a mental illness. It could look like that because of the fear and the shame and the hiding, but if people weren't so afraid, and kids could just be who they are, we might be able to skip the mental illness bit.*

- *This isn't a choice or fad that kids are pushed into. It's who they are.*

- *They have no right to know anything about anyone's gender that hasn't been shared with them by the individual.*

- *That it's not a choice a child makes. It's just who they are.*

- *It isn't a question of perversity or a phase … it is real … these people display a large heart, superhuman strength and courage to live the lives they knew they were born to be.*

- *It's really just a human experience. Start with that. Trans people are no different from anyone else. Just much more misunderstood.*

- *It isn't a choice, and they don't want to hurt other people. Many/ most trans people are hurting from negative experiences with hateful laws and policies.*

- *The anxiety and uncomfortableness they feel, all the time, in all situations.*

- *"Transgender" isn't a movement. Trans people are human beings just trying to live a normal, comfortable life.*

- *Kids with gender dysphoria are at risk of severe depression, anxiety, and even death if they don't get the support and acceptance they deserve.*

Contributors

THE STORIES AND POEMS ENCOMPASSED in this book beautifully reflect the diversity of the transgender community and the plethora of ways one can walk the path to authenticity. We are grateful to all who submitted stories and were thrilled to see the variety of ages, stages, and geographic locations of our contributors. Though all authors were given the option to be credited by name in the book, some have chosen to stay anonymous or only use a portion of their name.

Joy was written by **Alec Williams** (he/him), a parent and senior supervisor at a crisis intervention and suicide prevention hotline for LGBTQ+ youth in Kalamazoo, Michigan. Alec is also working toward a graduate degree in organizational leadership and social services and wants to encourage any trans reader to keep going, even on the hard days, because things will start to make sense someday in ways you never imagined possible.

My Name was written by **Avery Lewis** (he/they), a twenty-one-year-old college junior from Albany, New York. Avery is studying theater arts and one day hopes to be a playwright who creates meaningful pieces of theater to shed light on the trans experience. He loves to sing, sew, and cosplay. If Avery won the lottery, he would use the money to build a happy home for them and their partner, Ezra.

Enough Already, Crashing, and *The Name* were written by **B** (she/her), a parent from Virginia. She has loved writing and telling stories since she was a young child and is okay being comfortable in her discomfort because it means she's learning something. She loves her kid and is honored to be on this journey with her.

Staying Alive was written by **Bear** (they/them), a parent from Terra Haute, Indiana. Bear is known for their good humor, sense of fashion, and resilience. They love potatoes, the color lime green, and tabletop roleplaying games. Bear wants readers to know that trans youth are our future.

Living in the Gray Zone and *How Can I Protect You* were written by **Carol** (she/her), a parent and healthcare professional in the Washington, DC area who enjoys walking her dog in the woods and working on puzzles. Her heroes are the ordinary people who stand up for human dignity and respect, including parents of children with rare diseases and transgender kids who fight for their rights to use a bathroom, play on a sports team, and more.

Sex (Re)Education was written by **Chrissy Boylan** (she/her), a parent, writer, and yoga teacher from the greater DC area. She has been telling long stories since she was a child and loves being mama bear to all three of her children.

Seeing My Reflection was written by **Donnie Wilkie** (he/him), a nineteen- year-old college freshman from North Carolina, where he is studying biology, sociology, and creative writing. He loves dogs, horror movies, hiking, and trying new grocery stores or coffee shops. He credits his working-class, rural background in shaping who he is today.

Angel Wings was written by **Elena Chamorro** (they/them), a twenty-two- year-old independent film director from Chicago, Illinois, with a passion for social justice and environmental science. They like to read, write, bake, and cook and pride themselves on being eloquent, kind, and strong-hearted.

Choosing Myself and *Did I Disappoint You* were written by **Jackson** (he/him), a young adult and student in Leesburg, Virginia. Jackson is planning to major in English and has a passion for music, literature, and film. He also enjoys outdoor activities, including hiking, biking, horseback riding, and backpacking.

Statistic and *It Won't Happen Overnight* were both written by **Jay** (they/them/e/em), a seventeen-year-old high school junior just outside DC. Jay loves doing anything and everything creative, including but not limited to crochet, visual art, song-writing, poetry, world-building, and sewing. They want readers to know that they are an openly queer, disabled artist and athlete trying to make the world more just and liberated by living authentically and pursuing their passion as an activist.

School Days was written by **Jebediah** (he/him), a twenty-year-old young adult from California, where he is a second-year art major at University of California, Irvine. He also works as a museum art educator and loves his grandmother's paella, painting, and going to local punk and goth shows.

A Journey but So Much More was written by **Juli** (she/her), a parent and a biologist from Virginia. She's a hopeless optimist whose favorite time of day is dawn because it's the start of a brand new day, no doubt with coffee and time spent with her beloved horses.

Vessel was written by **Kai** (he/him), a nineteen-year-old assistant librarian who currently lives in Manchester, New Hampshire, and likes to read, play with his pets, and go to the gym. He thought firefighters were super cool when he was younger and believes kindness is the most radical thing we can do with our anger.

Redacted was written by **Lee** (he/they), a thoughtful, kind, seventeen-year- old high school junior from Tulsa, Oklahoma, with beautiful eyes. Lee participates in speech and debate, enjoys writing, and loves music. Lee's hidden talent is being able to identify and name most country flags! This is Lee's first published piece.

The Gift of Uncertainty was written by **Lisa** (she/her), a teacher and parent in the greater Washington, DC area. She has a great smile and sense of humor and loves to read or watch movies. She would be a full-time writer if she were to win the lottery, but in the mean- time, she chooses kindness as she continues to grow and learn as a person.

Fighting for the Future was written by **Max** (he/him), a nineteen-year-old college student at Virginia Commonwealth University studying social work and pre-nursing. Max loves mac and cheese and the color green. If he were to win the lottery, he would go on an epic shopping spree at a bookstore.

Leaving a Lifetime was written by **Moon** (they/them), a twenty-five-year- old community activist and linguistics teacher in Chattanooga, Tennessee, who loves anything with cheese, cuddling both their service dog and one-eyed cat, choreographing drag performances, and putting glitter on everything they own. They want people to know that Southern queers exist and thrive more than the news will tell you, and that their biggest strength is their tenacity.

To Those Who Pray was written by **Nile** (he/him), a high school senior from Lawrence, Massachusetts, whose favorite food is probably chicken tostadas but whose favorite book is *All Boys*

Aren't Blue by George M Johnson. He wants readers to know that he has no ill will toward anyone who is religious or believes in God, only those who use religion, specifically Christianity, as a shield for discrimination.

When Tomorrow Comes was written by **Owen Dempsey** (he/him), a young adult and special educator currently living in the Bay Area. He likes to surf, write music, go on road trips, play softball, and is in his trans joy era. He admires the trans people who came before him because they showed him that a future was possible and the trans kids who came after him who are unafraid to be themselves.

Not Just Another Hospital Stay was written by **Ray** (they/them), a seventeen- year-old high school student in Virginia who watches a lot of YouTube videos and loves their pet gecko.

Two Crescent Moons was written by **Ray JC Chang** (they/them), a twenty-year- old from Taipei, Taiwan, where they are studying food technology. They love activities that keep their hands busy, including crochet and origami, and want readers to know that they are still learning about their identity and gaining experience every day, and that's okay.

Just Embrace was written by **Rula Sinara** (she/her), a romance writer and parent in Virginia with a background in biology and allied health. She is passionate about organic gardening, wildlife and animals, reading, writing, cooking, and watching movies, and knows in her heart and mind that those in the trans community and beyond should be believed, supported, and protected.

He/They was written by **Seamus Ruth** (he/they), a twenty-year-old college student from Tampa, Florida. They are studying sociology and anthropology with a focus on folk studies. He is proud and deeply grateful for his Irish roots and is a passionate writer. He especially loves that they are what they are and wants us to know he is as human as anyone all over the world and throughout time.

The Runaway was written by **Stellan Knowles** (he/him/xe/xem), a twenty-two- year-old from Memphis, Tennessee, where he is the chair of the Memphis Youth Action Board. He prides himself on his dauntless- ness, his intelligence, and his determination to be true to himself and encourages all of us to be the authors of our own stories.

My Emerging Queerness was written by **Tia Sky** (they/them), a twenty-one- year-old student at Boston University studying sociology and community, power, and queer futures. They hope one day to run their own nonprofit organization and love bunny rabbits, reading, and watching TV.

TÖM (he/him) is a young adult currently living in Chicago, Illinois. He grew up in Indiana, singing and playing instruments with his musically inclined family, and continues to make music today. His favorite food is ramen noodles, his favorite color is red, and his favorite saying is, "The only way out of your feelings is through them."

We Say and *Roses and Roaches* were written by **Valerie Banks Amster** (she/her), a horse show announcer, children's songwriter, book editor and publisher, bookkeeper, Spanish tutor, and proud parent of a cisgender daughter and two transgender sons. She currently lives in Warrenton, Virginia, with her family, dogs, and a miniature horse.

My Gender Exploration was written by **a sixteen-year-old trans masc** from the greater Washington, DC area. They are a sophomore in high school and love bananas, the color green, reading, and watching TV.

Changes was written by **a neurodivergent queer thirteen-year-old** from the greater DC area. He likes to crochet and sew and also has a hidden talent for acting. Though they particularly like their sense of style and fashion, those who know him think it's his creativity, compassion, and individuality that make them so special.

(Gender) Message Received and *Taking T* were submitted anonymously.

Resources

Crisis Hotlines

Trans Lifeline – 877-565-8860

Trevor Lifeline – 866-488-7386

LGBT National Youth Talkline – 800-246-7743

LGBTQ National Help Center – 888-843-4564

National Runaway Safeline 24/7 – 1-800-786-2929

National Suicide Prevention Lifeline – 800-273-8255

General Information & Support

- **Gender Spectrum**: A variety of resources ranging from educational to religious to camps and sports, and policy resources.
- **It's Pronounced Metrosexual**: A free, online resource for learning and teaching about gender, sexuality, and social justice created by Sam Killermann.
- **Stand With Trans:** Provides education, advocacy, mentorship, and support for transgender youth and their families.
- **The Trevor Project**: A leading organization on combatting LGBTQ+ youth depression and suicide. They have educational resources, studies, and community support to learn about supporting your LGBTQ+ youth.

Teen & Parent Resources

- **It Gets Better**: A nonprofit organization with a mission to uplift, empower, and connect LGBTQ+ youth around the globe.
- **PFLAG**: A national organization with chapters across the US that hosts free support groups and activities for parents and teens.
- **TransFamily Alliance**: An educational space, resource hub, and support community for parents raising and supporting transgender, non-binary, and gender-expansive offspring.

- **Trans Youth Equality Foundation**: Provides education, advocacy, and support for transgender, non-binary, and gender non-conforming children and youth and their families.

School & Education

- **Gender Inclusive Schools**: Provides parent and educator training to proactively create safe learning environments for LGBTQ+ young people.
- **Genders & Sexualities Alliances (GSA)**: Student-led and student-organized school clubs that aim to create a safe, welcoming, and accepting school environment for all youth, regardless of sexual orientation or gender identity. (Formerly called Gay-Straight Alliance, they renamed to focus on gender and sexuality alliances).
- **GLSEN**: Founded by a group of teachers in 1990, GLSEN is an education organization working to end discrimination, harassment, and bullying based on sexual orientation, gender identity, and gender expression. and to prompt LGBTQ+ culture inclusion and awareness in K-12 schools.
- **Trans Student Educational Resources**: A youth-led organization dedicated to transforming the educational environment for trans and gender non-conforming students through advocacy and empowerment.
- **You Can Play Project**: An organization supporting transgender people wanting to play sports in their schools.
- **Welcoming Schools**: The Human Rights Campaign Foundation's Welcoming Schools program provides training to K-12 educators and youth-serving organizations around the country.

Trans Access & Advocacy

- **Advocates for Trans Equality:** A trans-led non-profit that provides gender affirming support and information on protection for trans rights.
- **Everything is Queer:** A worldwide map of over 10,000 queer-owned businesses and organizations. It has everything: toy stores, restaurants, LGBTQ+ massage therapists, and so much more.
- **Human Rights Campaign:** Focus on advocacy against policy, bills, and laws that discriminate against marginalized groups.
- **Transcend Legal:** Information about accessing trans-related healthcare.

*For state and local resources check out CenterLink LGBTQ+.

Acknowledgments

MOST OF THE EDUCATIONAL INFORMATION in this book comes from over a decade of Heather's dedicated focus working with gender-diverse youth and their families. However, we also sought and received input from several colleagues who have expertise in certain areas. For their substantial contributions, we want to thank Jessica Pavela; Liz Schnelzer, LCSW, CCI; Jennifer Glacel, LCSW, RPT-S; and Dr. Kori Saunders, PsyD, MA.

We must admit that when we started this project, we were a bit naive. We didn't think it would take over two years to pull it all together. But we also never imagined that awareness of the Trans Anthology Project (TAP) would spread through Instagram to all over the country and even overseas. We were originally hoping for about fifteen submissions to include in the book. We have included thirty-five. We expected most of the submissions to come from the teens and families Heather worked with directly. However, most have come from people neither of us has ever met. We expected the stories to be good, but they are truly *great*. We expected they would be diverse, but we grossly underestimated the degree of diversity in each person's account.

There are so many people who contributed to this project that we are wary of trying to list them all, lest we forget someone. However, we want to mention the following groups:

Instagram followers: Those who followed us on Instagram, shared posts, and responded to questions gave life to this project in significant ways. As the number of followers steadily climbed and the responses grew, we were fueled by the enthusiasm. Without our Instagram followers, we would never have reached across so many states and heard from people all over the country. Many thanks to all of you!

Our reading panel: Pamela Kirby, Tisha Moon, Jenna DeVore, and Sarah Braesch joined us for a long day of reading through all the submissions and evaluating them according to a rubric to determine themes and to assign each a writing coach for further development. Each of these people also took on the added time needed to connect with their assigned authors and help bring out the best in each piece. We sincerely appreciate their support.

Generous donors: The list below acknowledges the many generous donors who have contributed to the costs of publishing *Trans Anthology Project*. Special recognition goes to Jennifer Glacel, the owner and lead therapist at Seven Corners Psychotherapy in Falls Church, Virginia, who sent a generous check almost immediately after the Trans Anthology Project was first announced, long before there was any request for donations. Jennifer's check was unexpected and sent a message of support and confidence that invigorated our efforts. She subsequently sent two more donations, becoming one of the top donors for the project.

However, every single donation is greatly appreciated, not only for its monetary value, but also for its message to the trans community that there are hundreds of people who want to offer support, although the media doesn't often highlight these people.

Donors who contributed before this book went to print are recognized below.

PLATINUM Donors
Jennifer Glacel
Priscilla and Bill Kirby

GOLD Donors
Darcy Woessner
Heather Scott

SILVER Donors

Adam Gluck

Bob and Peggy McArthur

Casey Mitchel

Diane P. Scott

Liz Schnelzer

Luiza and Gordon Wilson

Michael Boylan

Norma McOmber

Stacy Baron

Stacy Evers

Stephanie Brown Howell

The Center For Family Wellbeing

Timothy Schuster

Advocates

Ami Lynch

Andrea Petersen

Anne Moyer

Ben Galison

Beth Roper

Brian Matthews

Cathy Simonte

Community of Faith UMC

Devon Combs

Elizabeth Dematteo

Erin Hill

James Simonte

Janet Forlini

John Palomino

Jorge Augusto Ramallo

Kari Koch - for Logan

Larissa de Graffenreid

Laura Grandy

Linda Walter

Margaret Klotz

Marta Hoilman

Martha Carpenter

Mikami Puchon

Mimi and Tucker Drummond

Nancy Casares

Nancy Graham

Natalie Goldberg

Pam Kirby

Rebecca Krouse

Robin Knoblach

Robyn Lady

Rula Sinara

Sally Patton and Mick Little

Sarah Bindbeutel

Sarah Young

Sati Yoga

Stephen and Laurie Chertock

Steve Simonte

Tait Sye

Tara Brill

The Tudor Family

Tisha Moon

TransFamily Alliance

Vinita Gotting

Valerie Hadeed

Allies

Abi Foerster

Doreen Fulton

Addison David

Emily Glidden

Alison French

Erica Thomas

Allison Goldfarb

Family Therapeutics

Allison Vess

Gregory Thomas

Amanda Van Emburgh

Heidi Carlson

Amy Cannava

Jane Hendrickson

Anne Ross

Jenna DeVore

Anonymous

Jessica Simon

Ashley DeCamp

Jessie Coleman

Asya Haikin

Jill Maguire

Barbara Gipe

Joe Cabush

Barbara Lavine

Julie Liddle

Barbara Shiff

Kathy and Richard Howard

Betsy Goodwin

Kelly Cregan

Brian Hasser

Kimberly Howard

Bridget Kraft

Kirsten Lundeberg

Carly Smith

Kristen Burton

Carolfina Yoga

Kristin Trombulak

Christina McCormick

Lisa Eidelkind

Crossroads Family

Lisa Howard

Counseling Center

Lisa Locke

David Paul

Lisa Tudor

Deborah Hertz

Mantell and Associates, LLC

Deborah O'Brien

Margaret Byrnes

Deborah Ross

Marissa Savage

Diane Ramira

Marsha Komandt

Acknowledgments

Mary Beth Lupoli

Mary King

Mary Martin

Matt Bebe

Meg Findley

Megan E Fellows LPC INC

Nanci Pedulla

Natacha Streiff

Nicolas Rosa

Patricia Commins

Pauline Schnelzer

Rebecca Rossiter

Rick Leichtweis

Shawn Rubin

Sherry Sposeep

Stephanie Brown - CF&C

Stephanie Shepperd

Steven Howard

Susan Anderson

Tanya Hull

Victoria Rose

Wendy Baird

About the
Authors

HEATHER H. KIRBY (she/her) is a therapist in the Washington, DC area with over twenty-five years of experience working with teens. She specializes in working with gender-diverse youth and their parents. She offers professional training and consultation to mental health providers interested in better supporting their gender-diverse

clients. Her first book, *Wild at Heart: Adolescents, Horses & Other Kindred Spirits*, won the silver medal in the Living Now Awards. Heather likes to remain active with horseback riding, hiking, gardening, and dog agility. She lives in Northern Virginia with her wife and two dogs.

CHRISSY BOYLAN (she/her) is a parent of a transgender young adult and writer whose work has appeared in the *Washington Post*, *The Christian Science Monitor*, *Life Lessons for Busy Moms: Essential Ingredients to Organize and Balance Your World* (*Chicken Soup for the Soul*), and several other publications. A graduate of the University of Michigan, Chrissy currently lives in Northern Virginia with her husband and three children.

Made in the USA
Middletown, DE
27 August 2024

59826840R00170